TWELVE KEYS TO
AN EFFECTIVE CHURCH
SECOND EDITION

BOOKS BY
KENNON L. CALLAHAN, PH.D.

Twelve Keys to an Effective Church, Second Edition,
Strong, Healthy Congregations Living in the Grace of God

The Twelve Keys Leaders' Guide, An Approach for Grassroots,
Key Leaders, and Pastors Together

The Twelve Keys Bible Study

The Future That Has Come

Small, Strong Congregations

A New Beginning for Pastors and Congregations

Preaching Grace

Twelve Keys for Living

Visiting in an Age of Mission

Effective Church Finances

Dynamic Worship

Giving and Stewardship

Effective Church Leadership

Building for Effective Mission

Twelve Keys to an Effective Church

Twelve Keys: The Planning Workbook

Twelve Keys: The Leaders' Guide

Twelve Keys: The Study Guide

TWELVE KEYS TO AN EFFECTIVE CHURCH
SECOND EDITION

Strong, Healthy Congregations Living in the Grace of God

Kennon L. Callahan

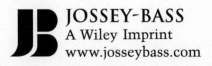

JOSSEY-BASS
A Wiley Imprint
www.josseybass.com

Published by Jossey-Bass
A Wiley Imprint
989 Market Street, San Francisco, CA 94103-1741—www.josseybass.com

Jossey-Bass books and products are available through most bookstores. To contact Jossey-Bass
directly call our Customer Care Department within the U.S. at 800-956-7739, outside the
U.S. at 317-572-3986, or fax 317-572-4002.

Jossey-Bass also publishes its books in a variety of electronic formats. Some content that
appears in print may not be available in electronic books.

Bible quotations are from the King James Version.

Library of Congress Cataloging-in-Publication Data
Callahan, Kennon L.
  Twelve keys to an effective church : strong, healthy congregations living in the grace of
God/Kennon L. Callahan. — 2nd ed.
      p. cm.
  Includes index.
  ISBN 978-0-470-55929-1 (cloth)
  1. Church renewal.   I. Title.
  BV600.3.C35 2010
  254'.5—dc22

                                                                                        2009038838

Printed in the United States of America
SECOND EDITION
HB Printing   10 9 8 7 6 5 4 3 2 1

CONTENTS

To Julia McCoy Callahan

Her life and love enrich our living together.

Her grace and compassion,
her wisdom and insight
are invaluable in advancing this new work.

Her gracious spirit and confident sense of hope
add richly to our lives together.
Warmly, with grace and love

KEN

A Prayer

Be at Peace . . . .

May the quiet grace of God restore your soul . . . .
  may good fun and good times find you,
    may your compassion stir you,
      may your wisdom bless you with insight,
        may new adventures give you
        new discoveries,
          may you live well,
            with integrity and honor.

Be at Peace . . . .

May you live with wonder and joy, grace and goodwill . . . .
  wonder that you are alive,
    joy that God blesses you with strengths,
      grace that God gives you compassion
      toward the universe,
        goodwill toward all beings
        with whom we share . . . .
          in this life and the next.

Be at Peace . . . .

May the grace of God bless you,
  the compassion of Christ sustain you,
    and the hope of the Holy Spirit lead you.

Amen.

Kennon L. Callahan, Ph.D.

....grace and peace to you from God....
ROMANS 1:7

Part One

THE BASIC QUALITIES

GRACE

I was helping a congregation. We were gathered in the
fellowship hall. The congregation had had twenty-five
losing seasons. They had slowly and steadily declined over
the years. We had shared a wonderful meal together. The
room was full. Leaders and grassroots had turned out in
droves. They saw this as a decisive gathering in the life
and future of their congregation.

One of the old-time mentor leaders, speaking on behalf
of the whole gathering, said, "Dr. Callahan, tell us about
the future of the Christian Church. We observe many
churches and many denominations in trouble. Our church
has been in trouble for years. Tell us about our future."

I had invested considerable time visiting informally with
many of the grassroots persons, key leaders, and the pastor
of the congregation. I had come to know their strengths,
what they have fun doing, some of their puzzles, their
history, and their hopes. I was impressed with the latent
strengths of the congregation.

"You have a strong future. Have this confidence and
assurance. We will have many strong, healthy congregations in the future. Your congregation has the latent
strengths, gifts, and competencies to be one of them."

I went on to say, "In the time to come, we will also have
many weak, declining congregations. We will have our
fair share of dying congregations."

With a gentle chuckle, Gene, the old-time mentor, said, "We have been doing pretty well at being weak and declining. We have had lots of practice. We almost have it down pat. A couple of times, over these recent years, we have almost made it to dying. We would like to try our hand at strong and healthy. We would be grateful for your wisdom and help."

"In the Outback of Australia, in West, West Texas, and in many remote places," I said, "it is tough to be a strong, healthy congregation. There are virtually no people. Wherever there are some people, a congregation can be strong and healthy. Some areas have fewer people than they did fifty years ago. But, they have more unchurched persons living around them now than they did back then."

Hopefully, Gene said, "You really think we have a future."

"Yes, Gene, your congregation can have a solid future. You can deliver the basic qualities of a strong, healthy congregation. And, you can deliver some of the twelve keys that contribute to a congregation being strong and healthy."

On a chalkboard, I drew a chart to help the grouping see the five basic qualities of strong, healthy congregations. We confirmed together that they have three of these five basic qualities well in place.

We took a good fun break. Tea, coffee, water, juice, fruit, cookies, sandwiches. Much laughter and good fun.

Then, we gathered to claim which of the twelve keys are their current strengths. We selected one current strength to expand, and one new strength to add. We acted swiftly.

Some little while later, Gene wrote me a personal note. He said, "We want to thank you. You have helped us to

get moving. You taught us how to think and behave like
a strong, healthy congregation. We have a ways to go yet.
We can see we will get there. Everyone thanks you."

BASIC QUALITIES

**Strong, healthy congregations share these basic quali-
ties: grace, strengths, compassion, excellent sprinters,
and act swiftly.** Healthy congregations deliver three of these
five basic qualities with considerable strength. With a diminishing spirit, weak, declining congregations share one or two of
these basic qualities. Dying congregations share one or none
of these basic qualities. You can assess where your congregation
is and where it is heading.

Strong, Healthy Congregations	Weak, Declining Congregations	Dying Congregations
live in the grace of God	sometimes know the grace of God	occasionally sense the grace of God
build on their strengths; then, tackle any weakness	focus on their weaknesses; then, address their strengths	focus on their weaknesses
compassion, community, hope; then, challenge, reasonability, commitment	challenge, reasonability, commitment; then, some compassion, community, hope	challenge, reasonability, commitment
excellent sprinter possibilities; some solid marathon runner possibilities	solid marathon runner possibilities; a few excellent sprinter possibilities	solid marathon runner possibilities
act swiftly	act slowly	study again

LIFE AND GRACE

Strong, healthy congregations share these basic qualities: grace, strengths, compassion, excellent sprinters, and act swiftly. Now, a word on behalf of grace.

Strong, healthy congregations live in the grace of God.

Life begins with grace. We are who we are through the grace of God. Everything in this universe and beyond begins with the grace of God. We are alive through the grace of God.

For strong, healthy congregations, life is a wedding feast of God's grace, a great banquet of God's hope. Life is filled with wonder and joy, sacrifice and service, and overflowing confidence and hope in the grace of God.

God blesses us with grace. Grace and life are good friends. Grace stirs life. Life stirs grace. We experience the grace of God and we find ourselves living whole, healthy lives. We share our longings for life and we discover, deeply, richly, the grace of God. The grace God gives us . . . . the life God gives us . . . . these are gifts of God.

We live in the grace of God even when we experience disappointments, despair, depression, despondency, death, sin, and worse . . . . In our time, people long for, yearn for, search for grace. They are less interested in organization, institution, and committee. They search for grace . . . . for the forgiving, loving, saving grace of God.

Grace is generous. God gives us the gift of grace so we can live grace-filled lives. The nature of grace is amazing generosity. "For God so loved the world . . . ." The Manger, the Life, the Teachings, the Cross, the Open Tomb, the Risen Lord . . . . these sacramental signs confirm the generous nature of God's grace.

Grace is grassroots. Jesus is born in a manger, not a mansion, a stable, not a castle, a cattle stall, not a cathedral. Shepherds and wise men gather, not princes and kings. Grace is for everyday, ordinary people who are born, live, and serve in mission, blessed by the grace of God.

Grace is gentle. Mission leaders have a spirit of humility. We discover our deepest humility in the presence of the grace of God. We become humility leaders. Grace is kind, and thoughtful. Grace is merciful, reconciling, and moving on.

Grace is mutual. Someone once observed that it is never quite clear who is really sharing grace with whom. The man in the ditch brings forth the best in a Samaritan, who in the centuries come and gone has been called Good Samaritan. Sometimes, the person we are helping is helping us to live our lives at our best . . . . in the grace of God.

Sometimes, we find grace. Sometimes, grace finds us. The gift of grace is not just a thing we do; it is a way we live. We are blessed of God. We are given this time. Our lives can count well, richly and fully, for the life of grace to which God encourages us.

GRACE AND CONGREGATIONS

God blesses congregations with keys of grace. Keys unlock doors. Keys unfasten gates. Keys open possibilities. The *Twelve Keys* are possibilities of grace. These keys help you to be strong and healthy. These keys are not mandates . . . . laws . . . . binding rules . . . . legalisms. They are not orders and obligations. It is not that each is *a should*, *a must*, or *an ought*. Rather, as possibilities, these keys open doors to being a strong, healthy congregation.

Growing a strong, healthy congregation is not, finally, a matter of data and demographics, graphs and charts, numbers and statistics. Nor is it a matter of the latest fads and foolishness, tricks and trivialities. Yes, we give attention to data and statistics. They have their rightful and proper place. We give more attention to the grace of God and the possibilities God gives us.

The *Twelve Keys* are possibilities of grace. You are welcome to approach them with a spirit of grace . . . . a theology of grace. They are keys. They open doors for the possibilities with which God is blessing your congregation. They are opportunities for you to develop a strong, healthy congregation, sharing richly and fully, in the grace and mission of God.

With these keys, you can grow a strong, healthy congregation. "Strong and healthy" and "effective and successful" are good friends. To be strong is to be effective. To be healthy is to be successful. In the spirit of grace, we focus on the strengths, gifts, and competencies of a congregation.

CONGREGATION AND FAMILY

You will discover that in this book, I use the term *congregation* frequently. The term encourages us to develop the relational life, the family spirit, the sense of community, of the congregation. A congregation is, finally, a family or a grouping of families with enough in common to share *the same spirit of grace* and the same informal leadership team of key leaders, volunteers, pastor, and staff. The term, congregation, confirms the person-centered, people-centered, relational dynamics of the informal family or families who are the congregation.

Frequent use of the word "church" draws people to an organizational, institutional perspective. A congregation is a family, a grouping or groupings of people gathered in the grace of God. We are not, finally, an organization or an institution. People, in our time, are not drawn to these. People are drawn to community, not committee.

We are drawn to a family, not an organization. The extended family clans that used to deliver this sense of family are scattered asunder across the landscape. We come to a congregation searching for home. When we find home, we help the family. We help the informal, person-centered grouping that is sharing healthy relations in the spirit of grace and family. We are a family of grace, compassion, community, and hope.

God's longing .... God's yearning is to share grace with us .... to stir us to grace and compassion, community and hope. God blesses us with grace .... gives us gifts for compassion .... invites us to live in community . . . . with hope. These are gifts of God. Through these gifts, we discover a life of grace. We live in grace.

GRACE AND STRENGTHS

To claim our strengths is to claim the grace of God. To deny our strengths is to deny the grace of God. The *Twelve Keys* books have contributed greatly to a major shift of the conversation from size to strengths. This shift is an important advance in the conversation. Now, we talk more of a congregation's strengths than its size. The mission growth movement focuses on strengths as gifts of the grace of God. It focuses on strengths for mission, not size. It is interested in advancing a strong mission of grace.

One mistake some people make, when they first look at the *Twelve Keys,* is that they ask, "Which ones don't we have; which ones are our weaknesses and shortcomings, which ones are our problems?" Some persons are too preoccupied with the problems, needs, concerns, weaknesses, shortcomings, difficulties, and dilemmas of congregations. Life itself has its fair share of these. When we focus first on our strengths, we are in the strongest position to deal with any weakness or shortcoming.

Regrettably, some see themselves as "fix it" persons. They look first for what is "broken" so they can "fix it." Their identity is wrapped up in "fixing things." They assume that their task is find what is weak and wrong and "fix it." They are preoccupied with finding "the problem" so they can bring "the solution." Sometimes, they try to fix what is not broken.

The art is to bless. Not fix. The art is *first* to bless and confirm with a congregation the strengths, gifts, and competencies with which God blesses them. We begin with God. We begin with God's grace. We begin with God's blessings. We begin with God's gifts. We look first for the strengths of a congregation.

The wise coach, first practice of the season, looks first for what we have going for us this year. Is this the year of power, blocking, and running? Is this the year of speed, quickness, and passing? The wise choral director, first practice of the season, listens for what we have going for us this year. Is it in the soprano, alto, tenor, or bass sections? In congregations, we look first for what we have going for us. And, the truth is that most congregations are doing better than they think they are.

We run to our strengths, not our weaknesses. We have a team with a pro center, pro right guard, pro right tackle, pro right end, and a pro right halfback. We would *not* run our plays around left end. We will get clobbered there. Yes, on occasion, we might pull a right guard and try a play in that direction. Yes, we would look for a pro left guard. That is, we would add new strengths that match with our current strengths. Mostly, *we run to our strengths*.

We sing to our strengths. We have a choir of pro sopranos, pro altos, and pro tenors. We sing music that matches with the strengths we have. We do not focus our music on the basses. We build our music repertoire on our strengths, not our weakness. Yes, we work toward improving the basses, but we would sing our *first* songs building on the sopranos, altos, and tenors. We go with, *we sing to our strengths*.

Congregations who first confirm the grace of God and claim their strengths, gifts, and competencies are viable and healthy, encouraging and developing. When a congregation focuses first on its strengths, it helps everyone in the congregation to focus first on their own gifts and strengths, in their own lives.

Strong, healthy congregations create strong, healthy persons.

Strong, healthy persons create strong, healthy congregations.

God invites us to focus on our strengths, not our size. Too much is made of size. When we develop our strengths, as gifts of the grace of God, we will be whatever size results from our strengths. The art is to grow stronger, not bigger. To be bigger is to be bigger, not necessarily better. Some people romanticize bigness. They focus on getting bigger. They say, "Thank God we are big and getting bigger." Some people do the reverse and romanticize smallness. They say, "Thank God, we are small and getting smaller." There is no merit either way. The merit is to experience the grace of God and to develop the strengths God gives you.

The term *strong* gives emphasis to the strengths, gifts, and competencies with which God blesses congregations. We are *effective* as we focus on our strengths. We become less preoccupied with weaknesses. We are encouraged, of God, to focus on our strengths.

The term *healthy* emphasizes that a strong congregation is a healthy family together. We encourage constructive relationships. We discover a sense of roots, place, and belonging together. We are a congregation of grace, compassion, community, and hope. We feel like family. We feel like home.

We have our fair share of difficulties and dilemmas, arguments and disagreements. The only groups I know who do not bicker and fuss, feud and argue are the people buried in the nearest cemetery. And, I am not always so sure about them. Sometimes, when I walk by late at night, I hear the mutterings and murmurings. What marks a healthy grouping of people is not the absence of conflict, but the presence of forgiveness, reconciliation, and moving on, with a healthy spirit of grace.

In tough times, we focus on the grace of God and the strengths with which God blesses us. In affluent times, in church culture times, in times when "it is the thing to do to go to church," we allowed ourselves, regrettably, the luxury and leisure of being preoccupied with our weaknesses. A focus on weaknesses *almost* works when times are affluent and easy. In these current times, in this mission culture, it is important, it is urgent that congregations live in the grace of God and build on their key strengths as they move forward in mission.

STRENGTHS

TWELVE ARE CENTRAL

Strong, healthy congregations share the basic qualities of grace, strengths, compassion, excellent sprinters, and act swiftly. Now, a word on behalf of strengths.

Strong, healthy congregations build on the strengths with which God blesses them.

Twelve possibilities consistently contribute to strong, healthy congregations. Yes, there may be fifteen to thirty to fifty characteristics that contribute to a congregation being strong and healthy, effective and successful. But, again and again, these twelve have tended to be persistently present in strong, healthy congregations.

In our research, wherever we find strong, healthy congregations, some of these twelve are present. These twelve are not so much a list of what a congregation should have. This is simply a listing of what strong, healthy congregations do have.

Feel free to consider fifteen to fifty characteristics of strong, healthy congregations. Look first at these twelve. You are welcome to look at other possibilities. Simply give your earliest consideration to these twelve. They are the ones consistently present in strong, healthy congregations.

For now, as you look at the chart, simply see the *Twelve Keys* for strong, healthy congregations. Later, you will have a fuller opportunity to consider which of these *Twelve Keys* are strengths in your congregation. I want you to have the benefit

Twelve Keys to an Effective Church
Strong, Healthy Congregations Living in the Grace of God

Relational Characteristics

1. one mission outreach
 by congregation in community
 1 2 3 4 5 6 7 8 9 10

2. shepherding visitation
 in congregation and community
 1 2 3 4 5 6 7 8 9 10

3. stirring, helpful worship
 grace centered, well done
 1 2 3 4 5 6 7 8 9 10

4. significant relational groupings
 home, roots, place, belonging
 1 2 3 4 5 6 7 8 9 10

5. strong leadership team
 leaders, pastor, staff
 1 2 3 4 5 6 7 8 9 10

6. solid decision process
 simple organization
 1 2 3 4 5 6 7 8 9 10

Functional Characteristics

7. one major program
 among best in community
 1 2 3 4 5 6 7 8 9 10

8. open accessibility
 in location and people
 1 2 3 4 5 6 7 8 9 10

9. high visibility
 in location and people
 1 2 3 4 5 6 7 8 9 10

10. land, landscaping,
 and parking
 1 2 3 4 5 6 7 8 9 10

11. adequate space and facilities
 spacious, well cared for
 1 2 3 4 5 6 7 8 9 10

12. generous giving
 solid financial resources
 1 2 3 4 5 6 7 8 9 10

Claim your current strengths
Expand one current strength
Add one new strength
Act on your plan

underline strengths (8s, 9s, 10s)
underline a second time
circle a 1–7 to grow to an 8
decide your one-time actions

of the **Twelve Keys** chart now so you can discover the central principles related to the **Twelve Keys.**

As you study each chapter, feel free to record your rating of each key on the **Twelve Keys** chart in Appendix C on page 258. Further, you can record your action plan and the key objectives you plan to achieve to strengthen your congregation. You will benefit from **The Twelve Keys Leaders' Guide** to help you develop your action plan.

For now, let's discover the **Twelve Keys.**

NINE OF TWELVE

Strong, healthy congregations deliver nine of the twelve. With one congregation, it will be a certain nine. With another congregation, it will be another nine. You deliver the nine that match best with your strengths and the mission field of persons God gives you.

You do not need all twelve.

One mistake people make when they look at the **Twelve Keys** chart is to ask, "Do we have all twelve?" That is simply that old, old friend, "a compulsive addictive perfectionism" showing up yet again in our lives. We learned that compulsive perfectionism somewhere, from someone or from several persons. Frequently, we learn it from someone who loves us and wants the best for us.

An interest in perfection is helpful, when we search for it in a relaxed, easygoing spirit, not too tense, not too tight, and not too anxious. Think of a golf swing. With a relaxed intentionality, we make a solid swing. It is when we think too much about the shot, try too hard, and seek to get it just right, that we make a bad swing.

The same is true with music. We want to be on key. We want to play the piece of music with perfection. When we have a relaxed and natural spirit, the music sounds wonderful. But, if we strive too hard, we become tense, tight, nervous, and anxious. We miss the note. We lose the beat.

In life, we want to do our best. We want to be growing toward perfection. But often, we try too hard. We do not let the grace of God help us. We try to earn what we have already been given. We seek to do it ourselves. We become tense, tight, nervous, and anxious. We become worried. We become preoccupied with "our efforts." We strive, without letting the grace of God help us.

The old, old rhyme was posted at the front of many classrooms. "Good, better, best. Never let it rest until your good is better and your better is best." The rhyme has a restless, striving focus. It is not relaxed and grace-filled. By contrast, at the end of a wonderful story, the angel says to the young couple, "Good, better, best. Know you are blessed." This is grace.

God invites us to grace, not law, to possibilities, not legalisms.

Compulsive addictive perfectionism, CAP, I sometimes call it, leads one to believe that all congregations should have the same characteristics, with the same strength, in the same manner, in order to be healthy and successful. By contrast, the *Twelve Keys* approach offers grace.

Congregations vary greatly. They have distinctive gifts, strengths, and competencies. There is a Biblical principle encouraging and blessing the diversity of gifts. A congregation does not need all twelve. Deliver the nine that match with your strengths and the mission field of persons God gives you.

Be at peace with three of the twelve. You will deliver nine of the twelve with considerable strength. Two things happen with the other three. One, you will be having so much fun delivering nine well that the other three will not matter. Two, your delivery of nine will be so strong that they create a spillover impact and some of the other three will come along on their own.

VALUE AND PRIORITY

In this book, the *Twelve Keys* are discussed in the order of their priority, value, and importance. For example, adequate parking is more helpful than adequate space and facilities. If you have a choice, have adequate parking and inadequate facilities. You will do better. I see too many congregations with adequate facilities and inadequate parking. They do less well.

If you have a choice, have open accessibility and, then, high visibility. You will do better. Too many congregations have high visibility, but lack accessibility. No one can find the church site. We can see the church site from the main road, but it is not clear how one gets to it. Lewis and Clark, or, for that matter, any of the early explorers, would take two years to find the site.

Significant relational groupings are slightly more important than a strong leadership team. The more new groupings you start, the more new leaders you will create. People who find home, help. Usually, they find their grouping first. Then, they volunteer. They pitch in and help. Start three new groupings that match with your mission, and, in time, you will have new volunteers and leaders. Some congregations beat the drum for volunteers without first trying to help persons find home. They wonder why they do not succeed in getting volunteers.

It is important to start new groupings that match with the mission of your congregation. These groupings will create new leaders that match with your congregation's mission. Thus, current leaders of your congregation's mission wisely help new groupings to be formed within, not apart from, the mission toward which your congregation is moving.

Shepherding visitation is slightly more important than dynamic worship. We have a pastor who is a good shepherd, loving and loved by the congregation. His sermon, rated a 7, will be heard as a 9. Not a good shepherd, the sermon will be heard as a 5. It is a whole lot more fun to be a 9 than a 5. It is in the shepherding, not the preaching.

Mission is slightly more important. Congregations who deliver one, major, helpful, legendary mission outreach do well. They live beyond themselves. They develop a theology of service, not a theology of survival. They develop a theology of mission, not a theology of maintenance. They help persons with their lives and destinies in the grace of God.

SOURCES OF SATISFACTION

The sources of satisfaction are: mission, shepherding, worship, groupings, leaders, and decision making. These are the relational, person-centered, people-centered characteristics of strong, healthy congregations. The more well in place some of these are, the higher the level of satisfaction in a congregation. Think of a barometer chart. With five of these six well in place, the level of satisfaction is very high on the chart.

The sources of dissatisfaction are: program, accessibility, visibility, land, landscaping, and parking, facilities, and giving. These are the functional, organizational, institutional character-istics of strong, healthy congregations. The more well in place some of these are, the lower the level of dissatisfaction. Think of another barometer chart. With four of these six well in place, the level of dissatisfaction is very low on the chart.

The strongest nine (see the *Twelve Keys* chart on page 13) are five of the first six—the relational characteristics—and four of the second six—the functional characteristics. We have a high level of satisfaction and we have a low level of dissatisfac-tion. Some congregations deliver three of the relational charac-teristics and have all six of the functional characteristics. Yes, this is nine. It is a weaker nine in our time.

In an earlier time, when it was a churched culture, congre-gations could "get away with" delivering primarily the func-tional characteristics. It was "the thing to do" to go to church in the culture of that time. Thus, congregations could pay less attention to the relational strengths, and people would still come to church. It was "the thing to do."

Going to church is no longer "the thing to do." Thus, in our contemporary culture the relational strengths are most impor-tant. Congregations that deliver five of these six thrive more

Sources of
Satisfaction

Sources of
Dissatisfaction

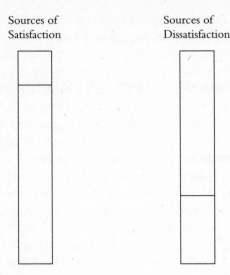

fully. This creates a high level of satisfaction. The higher the level of satisfaction, the more willing people are to "put up with" a source of dissatisfaction. For example, a congregation shares an extraordinary and helpful, stirring, and inspiring worship service. The result is that people are more willing to "put up with" inadequate parking.

Another congregation had a low level of satisfaction because it was not delivering some of the relational strengths. Also, it had a high level of dissatisfaction over inadequate space and facilities. They spent year one in the design of more adequate space and facilities. They spent year two in fund raising. They spent year three in construction. They moved in to adequate space and facilities. They lowered the level of dissatisfaction.

They did not raise the level of satisfaction one inch. They had worked on lowering the level of dissatisfaction. They had not raised any of the sources of satisfaction. A house does not make a home. People do. What, finally, raised the level of satisfaction was what began to happen *in* the new space and facilities: worship was now more stirring and inspiring and groupings now delivered a deeper sense of roots, place, and belonging.

Another congregation had been at a given location for ninety years plus. In that long lost earlier time, the location worked. The location had both open accessibility and high visibility. It was on the traffic patterns of the community. Time passed. Traffic patterns changed. The location was now a byway, hard to see, harder to find. People no longer drove by the church on their way to work, or shopping, or social and recreational events.

The congregation began to wither and die.

They voted three times over a thirty-year period on the issue of staying or moving, about once every ten years. The first vote and the second vote, over twenty of the thirty years, ended in a close margin to stay. The third vote, now with fewer people and weaker resources, was to move.

They spent three years. Year one—design. Year two—fund raising. Year three—construction. They achieved moving to an excellent location. There was a flurry of excitement and enthusiasm. The early time at the new location lived on these.

But they had assumed that the open accessibility and high visibility of the new location would bring people to them. And, it did. The hook was, they did not deliver any of the first four relational characteristics; mission outreach, shepherding, worship, or groupings. Note: they did not have to deliver all four of these. Two would do.

They made the mistake of assuming that a pretty new building at a splendid location would draw people. It did. It did not keep them. Two of the first four relational characteristics are what keep people. Thus, three years after moving in, after the euphoria and enthusiasm had waned, they found they were about where they had been in the long lost old location.

They put in place a swift action plan that helped them grow forward two of the first four relational strengths: shepherding visitation and stirring, helpful worship. They created a higher level of satisfaction. They became a strong, healthy congregation, a strong, healthy family. A house doesn't make a home. People do.

Think of your congregation. Consider your congregation's present and future. As you study the **Twelve Keys,** as you have conversations with persons in your congregation, keep in mind these principles:

Twelve strengths are central.

Strong, healthy congregations deliver nine of the twelve.

Each of the characteristics has a value and priority among the twelve.

In healthy congregations, the sources of satisfaction (the relational strengths) are stronger than the sources of dissatisfaction (the functional strengths).

Strong, healthy congregations share the grace of God and build on the strengths with which God blesses them.

COMPASSION

CONSTRUCTIVE MOTIVATIONS

Strong, healthy congregations share the basic qualities of grace, strengths, compassion, excellent sprinters, and act swiftly. We have spoken of grace and strengths. Now, a word on behalf of compassion.

Strong, healthy congregations share the motivations of compassion, community, and hope.

God blesses all of us with these constructive motivational resources:

Compassion	sharing, caring, giving, loving, serving
Community	good fun, good times, belonging, family
Hope	confidence, assurance in the grace of God
Challenge	accomplishment, achievement, attainment
Reasonability	data, analysis, logic, good sense
Commitment	duty, vow, obligation, loyalty

God blesses us with these resources. We draw on them. We motivate ourselves with them. They lead us to God; help us live whole, healthy lives; and help us serve well in the Christian movement.

All of these are present in every person. You can grow forward any of these. People tend to develop one or two as primary motivations at a given point in their lives. Life is a search . . . . a pilgrimage. Later, you might grow forward another of the motivations.

Motivation is internal, not external. These are the resources within a person with which the person motivates himself or herself forward. Thus, I refer to these six as the motivational resources with which God blesses us. God blesses us with grace, strengths, and motivational resources with which to grow forward a whole, healthy life. . . a strong, healthy congregation.

The Future That Has Come shares a rich, full discussion on these constructive motivational resources. Likewise, *Giving and Stewardship* and *The Twelve Keys Leaders' Guide* have excellent discussions of these motivational resources. For now, I want to confirm that healthy congregations share the motivations of compassion, community, and hope.

There are demotivators in life. Some of these are anxiety, fear, anger, rage, analysis paralysis, jealousy, despair, despondency, depression, and greed. We could develop an even longer list of the demotivators that distract us from the healthy motivations with which God blesses us. On occasion, we may find ourselves doing something out of one of these demotivators.

Frequently, anxiety leads to fear, fear to anger, and anger to rage. Despair, despondency, depression seem to go together. People with these demotivators do move, but they behave at less than their best true selves. They become tense, tight, nervous, and anxious. Under threat, people wither. With compassion, people grow. These demotivators lead us to our lesser selves. They seldom lead to constructive behavior.

MOTIVATIONAL MATCH

I am with many congregations who say to me, "Dr. Callahan, we want you to know we are experiencing solid worship attendance, our groupings flourish, we have many volunteers, and many people share generous giving." I immediately know I am with congregations who are sharing a motivational match.

In a congregation, all six motivational resources are present in the key leaders and the pastor. Two tend to be predominant.

All six are present with the grassroots of the congregation and the unchurched in the community. In a motivational match, the key leaders and pastor motivate themselves with any two of these three—compassion, community, or hope. This matches with the grassroots and the unchurched. They will be a strong, healthy congregation. See the chart "A Motivational Match in Strong, Healthy Congregations."

A Motivational Match in Strong, Healthy Congregations

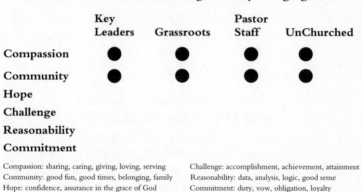

	Key Leaders	Grassroots	Pastor Staff	UnChurched
Compassion	●	●	●	●
Community	●	●	●	●
Hope				
Challenge				
Reasonability				
Commitment				

Compassion: sharing, caring, giving, loving, serving
Community: good fun, good times, belonging, family
Hope: confidence, assurance in the grace of God

Challenge: accomplishment, achievement, attainment
Reasonability: data, analysis, logic, good sense
Commitment: duty, vow, obligation, loyalty

There is a time for compassion. There is a time for commitment. This is the time for compassion. In this new time, we have seen a major paradigm shift from commitment to compassion. A healthy congregation lives with compassion. Its members have the confidence and assurance that one compelling way of reaching and growing the grassroots is thinking, planning, behaving, and living with the motivation of compassion. In a larger sense, in this new time, they share these three major motivations: compassion, community, and hope.

In an earlier time, a congregation could focus primarily on the motivations of challenge, reasonability, and commitment. In our time, compassion, community, and hope are more encouraging. Challenge, reasonability, and commitment are encouraging. Compassion, community, and hope are more encouraging. A strong, healthy congregation shares the motivations of compassion, community, and hope more than the motivations of challenge, reasonability, and commitment.

For the grassroots, ***compassion casting is more helpful than vision casting.*** Vision casting resonates with persons whose primary motivation is challenge. Wherever vision casting is working well, look closely; you will discover some person or persons who deliver compassion. Compassion is why people follow vision.

A strong, healthy congregation develops a motivational match between the key leaders and the grassroots, the pastor and the unchurched. A weak, declining congregation creates a motivational gap. A dying congregation makes the motivational gap wider.

MOTIVATIONAL GAP

I am with many congregations who say to me, "Dr. Callahan, we want you to know our worship attendance is meager, the same few people attend, the same few people do most of the work, and the same few people give most of the money." I immediately know I am with congregations who have a motivational gap.

Some key leaders and pastors motivate themselves with challenge, reasonability, or commitment. Regrettably, they assume that the motivations which stir them are the motivations that should stir the grassroots. They design recruitment projects and giving campaigns that focus on challenge thermometer goals, "reasonable" budget increases, and commitment Sundays. This resonates well with the key leaders and pastor. Year after year, they lament that the grassroots do not respond.

They broadcast on the motivational wavelengths (think of radio, wireless, satellite) of challenge, reasonability, and commitment. In committee meeting after committee meeting, the key leaders and the pastor say to one another, "If people were only more committed and could rise to the challenge, this blooming venture would get better." They resonate with one another, but they

A Motivational Gap: Weak, Declining and Dying Congregations

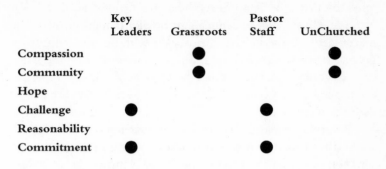

	Key Leaders	Grassroots	Pastor Staff	UnChurched
Compassion		●		●
Community		●		●
Hope				
Challenge	●		●	
Reasonability				
Commitment	●		●	

create a motivational gap with the grassroots and unchurched. They fail to see that the grassroots and unchurched have their frequencies tuned to compassion, community, and hope.

People share generously out of the motivations that stir in them, not out of the motivations that stir in someone else. The grassroots stir toward mission on any one of these—compassion, community, or hope. When we invite the grassroots to share in mission on one of these, we create a motivational match. Many volunteers emerge. Generous giving happens. Strong, healthy congregations move forward.

Context, sometimes, shapes behavior. It is interesting. A grandparent, with their grandchildren, behaves with compassion, like an excellent sprinter. The same person, in a church committee meeting, behaves with commitment, like a solid marathon runner. With the grassroots and the unchurched, we will do better when we behave like we do with our grandchildren.

In some instances, people have misapplied the "20-80" action principle to excuse the dilemma of weak, declining, and dying congregations. The 20-80 principle is simply this:

20 percent of what a group does delivers 80 percent of its results, accomplishments, and achievements.

80 percent of what a group does delivers 20 percent of its results, accomplishments, and achievements.

Vilfredo Pareto is the individual who researched and developed this principle. It has been widely used and is widely helpful.

Some have misapplied this principle, inappropriately and inaccurately, to the behavior of weak, declining, and dying congregations. In their misapplication, some suggest that 20 percent of the people do 80 percent of the work and give 80 percent of the money. They go on to suggest that 80 percent of the people do 20 percent of the work and give 20 percent of the money.

Pareto never meant either of those misapplications. Whenever we find a few people doing most of the work and giving most of the money, we have not found the 20–80 principle. *What we have found is a motivational gap.*

Regrettably, some congregations successfully create a motivational gap. Whenever the key leaders, the pastor, and the staff focus on any two of these—challenge, reasonability, commitment—they create, for their congregation, a motivational gap. The congregation becomes weak and declining.

Whenever the key leaders and the pastor—in a retrenching, retreating posture—seek to reinforce commitment and challenge, the motivational gap grows wider. Increasingly, the congregation moves from weak and declining to dying. The congregation dies because a few deeply committed, high-challenge leaders and a pastor work very hard on the wrong motivations.

The weak, declining congregation becomes a dying congregation. The key leaders and the pastor do not understand why this has happened. They rise to the challenge and deepen their commitment. They work even harder. As they do so, the motivational gap becomes wider and wider. They decline. They die.

COMPASSION AND COMMITMENT

The motivational resources list could have looked like this:

Compassion
Community

Hope
Challenge
Reasonability

I could have quit there. *I am for commitment.* It made the list.

What I am confirming is this: we are in a time of new beginnings. In a church culture, with an emphasis on institution, organization, and bureaucracy, one of the membership vows sounded like, "Will you be loyal to such-and-such denomination and support it by your prayers, your presence, your gifts, and your service?" In that church culture time, that commitment vow was an appropriate, fitting vow.

In the first century, there were no institutional membership vows. There were no denominations to which to be loyal. What was at stake was,

> "Will you love the Lord, your God, with all your heart, and mind, and soul, and strength?"
> "Will you love Jesus Christ as your Lord and Savior?"
> "Will you love your neighbor as generously as you love yourself?"
> "Will you live a whole, healthy life of grace, compassion, community, and hope?"

In our current time, what are at stake are these mission vows, not membership vows; movement vows, not institutional vows.

Many people say to me, "Dr. Callahan, what we need is people with more commitment." I usually say to them, "Good friend, you have just taught me you are a longtime Christian."

The early motivations that bring all of us to the grace of God, the compassion of Christ, and the hope of the Holy Spirit are the motivations of compassion, community, and hope. That early song is not, "Yes, Jesus is committed to me." The early song is, "Yes, Jesus loves me." The song "Amazing Grace" does not speak of amazing challenge or amazing commitment; it speaks of the amazing love and grace of God.

What happens is that we are drawn to the Christian movement out of compassion, community, and hope. Then, after
fifteen, twenty, or thirty years of living in the Christian life,
some people grow forward the motivation of commitment. Not
all do, but some do—particularly key leaders. The consequence
is that, for them, the important motivation that they believe
everyone should have is the motivation of commitment.

I invite them to think about the people who, many years
ago, helped them to become part of the Christian movement.
They talk about the sense of compassion, the spirit of community, the abiding presence of hope in these people.

I usually say to them, "What drew you, years ago, to the
Christian movement were the qualities of compassion, community, and hope. How could you expect to draw in the grassroots
and the unchurched with the motivations of challenge, reasonability, and commitment? That is not what drew you in. Why
would it draw them? And that was a churched culture time; this
is a mission field."

I invite them to share with me about their grandchildren.
They do. They have pictures. I encourage them to indicate to
me the motivations with which they share with their grandchildren. They speak of compassion, community, and hope.
I suggest that we relate to the grassroots and the unchurched
the same ways with which we relate to our grandchildren. Then,
we will do well with the grassroots and the unchurched.

At end of the movie *It's a Wonderful Life,* George receives
a small book, inscribed with these words: "George, No man
is a failure who has friends. Thanks for the wings. Clarence."
Compassion has wings.

Discipleship is compassion. This is especially true for people
new to the Christian movement. Jesus says to Peter, "Peter, do
you love me?" I honor the fact that discipleship is commitment. Many books are written on discipleship as commitment. Longtime Christians write them. The books simply teach
us that commitment is a motivation among some people *long*
in the Christian life. Compassion and commitment are good

friends. By itself, commitment is law, not grace. God invites us to grace.

Many congregations create a motivational match with the grassroots and the unchurched. They share the motivations of compassion, community, and hope. God blesses congregations that live with the richness and fullness of these motivations. These congregations are strong and healthy.

EXCELLENT SPRINTERS

GROWING

Strong, healthy congregations share the basic qualities of grace, strengths, compassion, excellent sprinters, and act swiftly. We have spoken of grace and strengths, and compassion. Now, a word on behalf of excellent sprinters.

Strong, healthy congregations develop a balance of excellent sprinter and solid marathon possibilities.

Excellent sprinters grow . . . . do what they do in one-time, seasonal, and short-term ways near the time at hand. Solid marathons runners grow. . . . do what they do in steady, weekly, monthly ways, year in and year out. These are learned patterns of behavior. No one is born genetically one way or the other. You can learn both patterns of behavior. You are welcome to benefit from my discussion of these possibilities in my book *The Future That Has Come.*

Solid marathon runners pack for vacation three weeks ahead and have checked it four times. Excellent sprinters pack for vacation as the car is leaving the drive. They both have fun on the same vacation. Marathoners study two hours every night. Sprinters study two nights before the exam. They both do well on the test.

For now, I want to confirm that it is easier to grow a strong, healthy congregation when one is growing a healthy life. When we learn to lead our lives, we find it easier to lead a congregation.

If you can lead only one person, lead yourself. It is easier to lead others when one is learning to lead one's self.

We seek a growing, developing life. Some of us grow as excellent sprinters, in short-term, highly intensive ways near the time at hand. Some develop as solid marathon runners, in routine, regular ways, weekly, monthly, year-round ways. Many have learned both patterns of behavior. Thus, with both patterns of behavior available, we select the pattern helpful for the task at hand.

Many grandparents have learned both patterns. They learned a solid marathon pattern of behavior in their growing-up years and in their middle years. The marathon culture of that earlier time reinforced that pattern of behavior.

They experience the gift of grandchildren.

The grandchildren help them to learn an excellent sprinter pattern. The excellent sprinter culture of this present time encourages, confirms this behavior pattern. They rejoice in their grandchildren. They rejoice that they now have two behavior patterns to help them grow forward.

We grow forward. . . . we develop and advance in these ways:

One-time
Seasonal
Short term, in three to five sessions
Long term, six or more sessions
Weekly, monthly, year round

Excellent sprinters grow their lives in one-time, seasonal, and short-term ways. Solid marathon runners do so in long-term and weekly, monthly, year-round ways. Persons who have learned both behavior patterns grow in all of these ways.

Many persons grow in one-time ways. Alcoholics Anonymous is a major movement. People learn to live healthy lives—one day at a time. No one gives up drinking for life, or even weekly, monthly, year round. They give it up one day at a time. Emmaus Walk, Promise Keepers, revivals, camps, retreats, mission projects, and seminars are one-time ways people grow forward their lives. Countless millions of people benefit from these excellent sprinter ways of growing their lives.

Habitat for Humanity is a one-time approach to mission. People come. . ... build one house. Some have helped build one house every year over eight years. But they never "signed up to build a house every year." They signed up—one time—to build one house. They had so much fun, gained so much satisfaction; they signed up to build one house again. Looking back, they are surprised to see they helped build eight.

Strong, healthy congregations offer many one-time, seasonal, and short-term possibilities. More persons participate. Generous giving happens. Many people help. Many people are helped. The art of growing a healthy life and growing a strong, healthy congregation is the same.

CULTURE

In Toffler's book **Future Shock,** he identifies the stages of human civilization: nomadic, agrarian, industrial, and technological. I advance Toffler's research.

Toffler	*Callahan*
Nomadic	Marathon
Agrarian	Marathon
Industrial	Marathon
Technological	Sprinter

Two events have happened in our time: the shift from an industrial culture to a technological culture . . . . and the shift from a marathon culture to an excellent sprinter culture.

In the nomadic culture, we followed the herds, the water, and the seasons in routine, regular ways year after year. In the agrarian culture, we watched the growing of the crops in routine, regular ways year after year. There were two sprints, planting and harvest, but it was mostly a marathon time. In the industrial culture, we manufactured "x" number of widgets per day, per week, per month, year in and year out in a routine, regular way. There may have been a "peak season" from time to time. Mostly, it was a marathon culture pattern.

An excellent sprinter culture reinforces key objectives, short-term projects, and quick, highly intensive patterns of behavior. I have always known that many persons are solid marathon runners, many persons are excellent sprinters, and many persons have learned both patterns of behavior. In an earlier time, the culture reinforced marathon patterns. In our time, the culture reinforces excellent sprinter patterns of behavior.

What has changed is the pace, not the busyness. In an earlier time, people were busy running five marathons. In our time, people are busy running five excellent sprints. Life moves quicker, faster, with many short-term projects. Amazingly, many people have become excellent sprinters.

In that earlier time, the parable taught that the tortoise won the race. The parable was an invention of a marathon culture to reinforce, that if you want to get down the yellow brick road of life and meet the Wizard of Oz, you will behave in slow, steady ways. In our time, the hare wins. The tortoise finishes the race. The hare wins.

In an earlier time, seven of ten children were marathon runners and three were misfit excellent sprinters. In our time, seven of ten children are excellent sprinters. Grandparents discover this quickly. They thrive. Their grandchildren thrive. Grandparents say, "If we knew how much fun grandchildren were going to be, we would have had them first."

POSSIBILITIES FOR BALANCE

First, look at the people you are seeking to serve. When you discover that the majority of them are excellent sprinters, encourage people to create many excellent sprinter possibilities. In an earlier time, we looked and saw that the majority were solid marathon runners. We created marathon possibilities. It worked. In our time, a *balance* of possibilities frequently looks like this chart.

Ways People Live Life

Home, Roots, Place, Belonging, Friends, Family

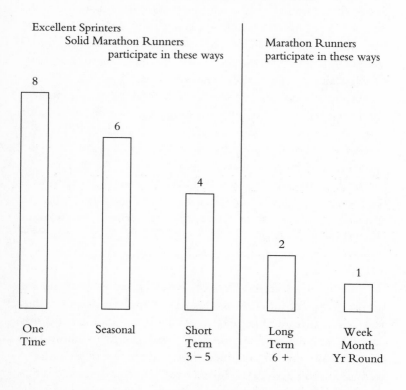

Excellent Sprinters
Solid Marathon Runners
participate in these ways | Marathon Runners
participate in these ways

8 — One Time
6 — Seasonal
4 — Short Term 3 – 5
2 — Long Term 6 +
1 — Week Month Yr Round

We have eight one-time possibilities, six seasonal possibilities, and four short-term groupings. We have two long-term possibilities and one weekly, monthly, year-round possibility. We match the range of persons God gives us. We are a strong, healthy congregation.

A Chart of a Weak, Declining Congregation

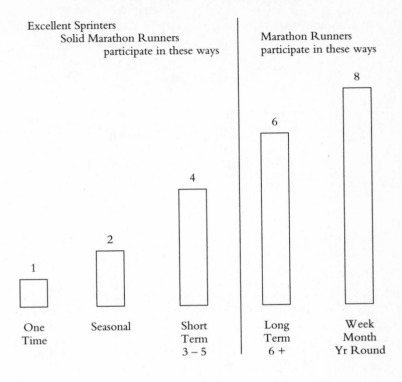

Excellent Sprinters
Solid Marathon Runners
participate in these ways

Marathon Runners
participate in these ways

8

6

4

2

1

One
Time

Seasonal

Short
Term
3 – 5

Long
Term
6 +

Week
Month
Yr Round

We have eight weekly, monthly, year-round possibilities and six long-term possibilities. We have four short-term possibilities, two seasonal possibilities, and one one-time possibility. Mostly, we use the one-time, seasonal, and short-term possibilities as "bait." When people join, they are taught, "Now that you are a member, we count on you, expect you to become a solid marathon runner and participate in long-term and weekly, monthly, year-round possibilities and volunteer activities." It is a "bait and switch." We are on our way to creating a new inactive member.

We have eight weekly, monthly, year-round possibilities and six long-term possibilities. We have no short-term possibilities, no seasonal possibilities, and no one-time possibilities.

A Chart of a Dying Congregation

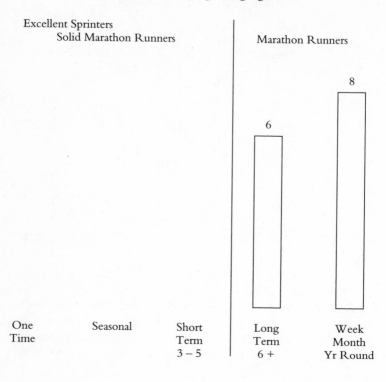

The stubborn, habitual notion is that "what worked years ago will work now." Yes, it worked. It would work still in a solid marathon culture, a church culture, and an institutional culture. It would work wherever the persons we seek to serve are solid marathon runners.

We live in an excellent sprinter time. Congregations are strong and healthy as they develop a balance of excellent sprinter and solid marathon runner possibilities.

ACT SWIFTLY

HAVE FUN

Strong, healthy congregations share the basic qualities of grace, strengths, compassion, excellent sprinters, and act swiftly. We have spoken of grace, strengths, compassion, and excellent sprinters. Now, a word on behalf of act swiftly.

Strong, healthy congregations act swiftly.

When we are having fun, we are more likely to act swiftly. What we have fun doing is God's way of teaching us our strengths . . . . our longings . . . . our yearnings . . . . our mission. We live life more richly and fully when we are having fun, in the deepest sense of grace-filled fun.

We develop better action plans when we are having fun. When we are too solemn and too serious, we become tense and tight, nervous and anxious, afraid to make a mistake. We *over plan* and end up doing nothing. When we *under plan*, we are more likely to head to the action, to doing something worthwhile.

In the Bahamas, the water is shallow in many places. There are sand bars and coral reefs abounding. Most sailors, on occasion, run aground. The saying is, "The skipper who says he has never run aground, his boat has never left the dock."

When people become tense and tight, they create too much of a plan, with too many objectives, set too high, to be accomplished too soon. They intuitively sense they have set themselves up to fail. They become fearful of failure. They postpone action to postpone failure.

The problem is not procrastination. The deeper problem is perfectionism. They have too many objectives, set too high, to be accomplished too soon. The best way to *not* fail is to never do anything, to never leave the dock. The action plan sits on a shelf. The boat stays at the dock.

When people are relaxed and having fun, they create almost enough of a plan, with a few key objectives, realistic and achievable, with solid time horizons. They intuitively sense they have set themselves up to succeed. They set sail. They act.

As people are having fun, with a spirit of grace and discovery, and are enjoying good times together, they develop a clear sense of their current strengths. Yes, be thoughtful, but not too serious. When we become too analytical, too serious, we talk ourselves out of our strengths, gifts, and competencies.

We look forward to the grace of God, inviting and encouraging us. We want our action plan to make sense . . . . to make *some* sense. *But, if we did things based on them making complete sense, no one would be married.* No one gets married because it makes sense. People get married out of compassion, community, and hope. Then, they rationalize why it made sense to get married earlier rather than later.

Congregations are like people. The art is to build on the strengths with which God is blessing you, to build on your passion and compassion, to build on what you have fun doing, to rejoice in God's gifts, to build on the grace of God.

PRAY

When we are praying, we are more likely to act swiftly. When we pray, we have fun. We pray with gratitude for the life God gives us . . . . for the grace with which God blesses us . . . . for the strengths God gives us. We pray with thankfulness for God's stirring, moving, living presence in our lives.

We pray that God will stir our hearts . . . . deepen our compassion . . . . draw us close together as community . . . . as family.

We pray God will give us wisdom and judgment, vision and common sense. We pray God will surround us with joy and peace, assurance and hope.

We pray God will be with us as we read this book and as we share in conversations together about our present and our future. We pray we will discover excellent ideas and good suggestions . . . . insights and possibilities . . . .

We have confidence in the grace of God. We know our future is in God's hands. Yes, we will be thoughtful with data and demographics, charts and graphs. We will set aside gimmicks and gadgets, tricks and trivialities, the latest fads and foolishnesses. We will trust in the living, stirring grace of God as we grow forward.

CLAIM

When we claim our strengths, we are more likely to act swiftly.

Claim your strengths, gifts, and competencies . . . . with wonder and joy, humility and gratitude. Your strengths are gifts of God. It is through the grace of God, the generosity of God that you have whatever strengths and competencies you have. God has been moving, stirring, living, working in your life, in your congregation, encouraging, helping, and giving. The results of God's grace are the gifts, strengths, competencies which you have.

If you can do only one thing that will help your congregation, it is to claim your strengths.

We claim our strengths. We rejoice in the grace of God. We give thanks for God's gifts. Yes, we do a thoughtful analytical study of our current strengths. We do more. We are grateful, deeply, fully, humbly, to God for the strengths we have. We give thanks to God for God's grace and gifts in our lives, in our congregation. We rejoice in God's blessings!

Some people spend half their lives devaluing and diminishing themselves, thinking more poorly of themselves than they have a right to, suffering from low self-esteem. They deny their strengths. They deny the grace of God. They deny God's gifts. They deny God.

Some congregations do the same. They look down on themselves. They become preoccupied with their needs and concerns, problems and difficulties, weaknesses and shortcomings. They deny their strengths. They deny the grace of God. They deny God's gifts. They deny God. The sadness is that most congregations are doing better than they think they are.

In life, the art is to claim our strengths. When we claim our strengths, we claim the grace of God. Yes, when we claim our strengths, we have a more solid sense of self-esteem. This sense of confidence and assurance helps us in living whole, healthy lives. More important, claiming our strengths is a matter of grace, of confirming that whatever gifts, strengths, and competencies we have, we have as gifts of God's grace.

Instead of claiming their strengths, some people are too preoccupied with addressing their weaknesses and shortcomings. Perhaps, (1) they want to be helpful, but their desire to be helpful can overcome them. Their desire to help draws them to weaknesses. They deliver more help than would be helpful. They do harm in the end. They create a pattern of dependency and co-dependency.

Some people (2) suffer from a compulsive addictive perfectionism. They are drawn to "fix it." Tidy it up. Make it look better . . . perfect. With some, (3) their low self-esteem draws them to weaknesses and shortcomings. With some, (4) their well developed gift for scolding leads them to weaknesses. With a preoccupation on weaknesses, they can scold, in a low voice, quietly, firmly, and fully.

Meister Eckhart had a saying, "The devil has a device called busyness with which he tries to convince Christians they are really doing the will of God." My saying is, "The devil has a device called weaknesses with which he tries to lure Christians from the strengths God gives them."

C. S. Lewis, in the *Screw Tape Letters,* writes of persons "being eternally distracted."

Strong, healthy congregations live in the grace of God. They claim their strengths, gifts, and competencies. They do not think more poorly of themselves than they have a right to. They do not think better of themselves than they have a right to. They have a realistic assessment of their strengths. They claim their competencies.

We look for the strengths we have, not the ones we wish we had. When we look for the strengths we wish we had, we miss the strengths we really have.

One of my players, Bob, all season long, kept jumping up and down, "Coach, let me pitch, let me pitch, let me pitch." After a while you get tired of the pleading and whining. In one game, toward the end of the season, I started him as pitcher. We were still in the first inning. The other team was having a field day at bat. Bases loaded. No outs. We were nine runs behind.

One of the hardest things I have ever had to do was walk out to the pitcher's mound, in what I hoped would be near the end of the first inning. I said to Bob, "This is my fault. This is my mistake. I should have been out here five runs ago. You are our best shortstop. Please, now, go play shortstop. Sam is coming in as pitcher. With your fielding, the rest of the team's fielding, and Sam's pitching, we will get out of this inning and beyond this game." We did.

Another season. Another team. An important game. I started John as pitcher. We were in the first inning. The other team had men on all three bases. There were no outs. We were now four runs behind. I said to myself, "I've been here before." I called a time out. I walked to the mound. John was glad to see me coming. He was not eager to continue. As I drew near, John started to step off the mound. He handed me the ball.

I handed the ball back to him. I said, "John, I don't know what in the name of heaven you think you are doing out here, but you had better figure it out pretty quick, because you are the only one who is going to pitch this whole game." He did. He pitched himself out of the inning. He pitched the whole game. With confidence and assurance. We won by one run.

Bob's gifts are at shortstop. John's gifts are at pitcher. God blesses both.

The art is to build on the strengths you have, not the ones you wish you had. Bob had spent too much time preoccupied with the gift he wished he had, and not enough time on the gift he has, namely, playing shortstop. John was about to give up on his real gift, pitching. With encouragement, he came into his own. He became our best pitcher.

The art of claiming your strengths is a matter of theology. We do not claim our strengths so we can think better of ourselves. It is not finally a matter of self-worth, self-esteem, or positive thinking. It is not finally rooted in us. We are claiming the grace of God in our lives. We live a theology of grace. We claim our strengths as a matter of grace.

> *For by grace, are ye saved through faith; and that not*
> *of yourselves; it is the gift of God.*
> Ephesians 2:8 (KJV)

I understand the text to include this spirit . . . .

> *For by grace, we are given these strengths;*
> *and these are not of our own doing; they are gifts of God.*

We begin with our strengths. We claim. We expand. We add. We sustain. We act swiftly.

Then, we are in the strongest position to tackle a weakness. When we begin with a weakness, we are in the weakest position to tackle a weakness. In this book, we will not ignore weaknesses, but we will not begin with weaknesses. We will begin with God. We will begin with the strengths God gives you. You are a person, a congregation, with gifts, strengths, and competencies.

One way to deal with a weakness is to "let go of it." Feel free to give yourself liberating permission to "let go" of a weakness. Many of our weaknesses have power only because we give them power over us. Grudges, resentments, bitterness, self-defeats, anxieties, and more have power over us because we give them power. The harder we work on them, the more power we give them. The text in Hebrews 12:1 is helpful: "Since, therefore, we are surrounded by so great a cloud of witnesses, let us let go (lay aside) every weight, and sin which clings so closely . . . ."

First, we claim our strengths. We give thanks to God. We rejoice in God's gifts.

EXPAND

When we expand one or two of our current strengths, we are more likely to act swiftly.

It takes wisdom, judgment, vision, common sense, and prayer to claim our current strengths. It takes more of these to decide which one of our current strengths to expand. The art is to take an 8 on a scale of 1 to 10 and grow it forward as a 9 or 10.

If you could do a second thing that will help your congregation, it is to expand one of your current strengths.

We do better what we do best. We build on our strengths, not our weaknesses. We select a current strength to grow forward. We pick one that is an easy, highly visible, quick win. We choose a current strength that is the simplest to grow forward. We do not consider one that we think we "should" grow forward. We stay away from one that we think we "ought to" grow.

We select one current strength we would have fun growing.

The art is to match the plays with the players. We send in plays the players can run, not plays someone thinks they "should" run. We can learn some things from what other congregations are doing. We can benefit from their successes and from their excellent mistakes. But, simply because something works well somewhere else does not mean it will work with us. With wisdom and prayer, we select a strength we can expand.

We never send in more plays than the players can run. Some congregations have too big, too thick of a playbook.

They do the cafeteria approach to long-range planning. They think of almost everything that everyone in the congregation can suggest for possible, probable, maybe inclusion in a "long-range" plan.

They gather all of these suggestions and ideas into a ninety-seven-page "long-range" plan. It does two things well. One, it sits on a shelf that would otherwise be empty and lonely. Two, it gathers dust that we would have to gather in some other place in the galaxies.

We expand one current strength, maybe two. We focus on what we can deliver, simply and graciously. We bring our wisdom and judgment to bear. We have a sense of vision. We use our common sense. We pray. We have fun. We move forward.

ADD

When we add one or two new strengths, we are more likely to act swiftly.

If you could do a third thing that will help your congregation, it is to add one new strength.

Look for the central characteristics, among the **Twelve Keys,** that are "mid-range" strengths. On a scale of 1 to 10, these are a 5, 6, or 7. We do not select our weakest weakness, something that is a −49 on a scale of 1 to 10. We look for a possibility, among the twelve, that has promise of becoming a new strength.

A congregation is a grouping of people, blessed with the grace of God. Congregations do not have precisely the same set of strengths. Congregations do not add the same strengths. In the New Testament, we discover these words:

> *Now there are diversities of gifts, but the same Spirit.*
> I Corinthians 12:4 (KJV)

No two congregations are exactly the same. A congregation adds the distinctive strengths with which God blesses it.

Music groups play the same piece of music in distinctive ways. The Biblical principle is a diversity of gifts. As you select a key to add as a new strength, you are welcome to look at what other congregations are doing and to learn from them. Mostly, look at what you would have fun doing, what matches with your current strengths, and what would be helpful in the community in which you serve in mission.

Should you discover three or four keys you would have fun adding, select one or two, for now. Save the others for the time to come.

SUSTAIN YOUR CURRENT STRENGTHS

When we sustain our current strengths, we are more likely to act swiftly.

If you could do a fourth thing that will help your congregation, it is to sustain your current strengths.

Strong, healthy congregations expand one current strength and add one new strength. They also sustain their other current strengths. They do not become preoccupied with the one current strength they are expanding and the one new strength they are adding. They do not neglect the other strengths they already have well in place.

Sometimes, the gift of encouragement will sustain your current strengths. Sometimes, one key objective well achieved will sustain a current strength. What we would not do is withdraw leaders, volunteers, staff, and funding that have made this a strength for our congregation. What we would not do is neglect what we have already built.

One congregation decided it would add a new strength, the seventh central characteristic—one major program. They already had a strength in the third central characteristic—stirring, helpful worship. But to bolster their new add, they diminished the staffing and money they had been investing in worship. Instead, they invested it in program. They ended up gaining a new strength in program and losing a current strength in worship.

The art is to sustain your current strengths.

ACT SWIFTLY

When we act swiftly, we are more likely to be a strong, healthy congregation.

If you could do a fifth thing that will help your congregation, it is to act swiftly on your present and future.

When we live in the grace of God, we are more likely to act swiftly. The best action plans are swift, simple, and stream-lined. We act now.

We act swiftly, with speed. We look three weeks, three months, and three years ahead. Sometimes, looking three weeks and three months ahead is sufficient for the present time. You are wel-come to see how this three-month time line lives itself out in *A New Beginning for Pastors and Congregations.*

The art is to work smarter, not harder. The art is to focus, not to be busy. Congregations become strong and healthy through compassion and wisdom, not through a merry-go-round of busy, bustling activities. Some congregations suffer from "80 percenteritis." They become preoccupied with every little mat-ter around. They redouble their efforts on the 80 percenter objectives. They intuitively know these only achieve 20 percent of the results.

Healthy congregations focus well on a few keys, possibili-ties, and objectives. Busyness, coupled with working harder, does not help. In a healthy congregation, we expand one or two current strengths. We add one or two new strengths. We sustain our current strengths. We work smarter. *The art is to work swiftly, not slowly.* We act swiftly.

We have the capacity to act swiftly. I am amazed at how well people pitch in and help in a disaster. I have the privilege of sharing and working with the Salvation Army. The Army is among the best groupings at delivering relief in a disaster. I greatly admire what they achieve. Over the years, I have come to several insights about the behavior of persons in a time of disaster.

In disaster relief, we are at our best. We rise to the cause. We deliver.

1. Our spirit of *compassion* is compelling, richly present, and generously given. We help in a disaster out of compassion, not challenge, reasonability, or commitment.
2. Our *focus* is on the disaster. We are not trying to do everything. We do not allow ourselves to be distracted by many other things. We have an intense focus on one major project: the disaster.
3. We have a *flexible* spirit. We look for the possibilities that will help. Each disaster has its own distinctive character. With much flexible and mutual teamwork, we match the disaster with what works for the specific disaster.
4. We move, *swiftly* . . . . with speed. We run. We are excellent sprinters in a disaster. There is no time for being a solid marathon runner. We are fast in delivering help. There are no long committee meetings. There are no long, long detailed discussions. The disaster is upon us. We sprint.

We can learn from what we do well in the time of a disaster. Some congregations, regrettably, try to grow forward with the motivation of commitment, doing many programs, in a rigid, planned way, with a slow, solid marathon runner pace. These behavior patterns do not work in a disaster. We have tried them in normal times. They do not work there. If they did, we would be better off.

Sometimes, I think we would be better to see our congregation as a disaster. In the best spirit, we would mobilize the behaviors we do so well in times of disaster. We share compassion. We have focus. We are flexible. We have an excellent sprinter spirit. We act swiftly.

Now, most congregations have solid strengths. Most congregations are doing better than they think they are. I am not suggesting that you actually view your congregation as a disaster. Nor am I suggesting you manufacture a false disaster. I am suggesting we learn from the behavior patterns we share so well in a disaster.

We have the capacity to act swiftly. If we can do these behavior patterns in a time of disaster, we can learn how to apply them to growing a strong, healthy congregation. Compassion. Focus. Flexible. Excellent Sprinter Spirit. Swiftly. We head to the Action. We grow. We thrive. We do well. We are strong and healthy.

LIVING AND ACTION

We act. We live. Many congregations do these two things well. *One, we act on excellent key objectives.* We claim our strengths. We expand one current strength. We discover two to four few key objectives to do so. We add one new strength. We discover four to six key objectives to do so. We sense God encouraging us to expand this current strength, to add this new strength.

Two, we live the basic qualities of strong, healthy congregations. We have excellent objectives. We go about achieving them with the basic qualities. It works. We do two things well. We have excellent objectives. We go about achieving them in a healthy way.

For example, we decide to expand our current strength in worship. We discover four key objectives to do so. *How we head toward these objectives is as important as where we head.* The basic qualities of strong, healthy congregations shape how we head toward these key objectives . . . . with a spirit of grace

we focus on our key objectives in worship
we build on our specific strengths in worship
our motivation of compassion stirs us
we move forward with an excellent sprinter spirit
we act swiftly

We do not head toward these key objectives with the qualities of weak, declining or dying congregations. We do not have a spirit of law. We are not preoccupied with our weaknesses. Demotivation does not creep in. A sluggish approach does not overcome us. We do not act slowly.

Some congregations have excellent objectives but go about achieving them in a lesser way. They fail. They fail, not because the objectives were wrong. The objectives were fine. But they went about them the wrong way.

The basic qualities of strong, healthy congregations inform and shape how we move forward on our key objectives. We focus on the key objectives we plan to achieve. We focus on how we plan to achieve them. Where we head and how we head there reinforce one another. The key objectives are decisive. The spirit with which we achieve them is decisive.

We grow forward the key objectives to which God invites us. As we do so, we live these basic qualities: grace, strengths, compassion, excellent sprinters, and act swiftly. These basic qualities are the spirit with which we move forward. We act in the grace of God. We live in the grace of God.

We live. We act. We live with a spirit of grace. We act on our present and future, building on the strengths with which God blesses us. Our strengths, gifts of God, are sacramental gifts, to be respected and treasured. We live and act with compassion . . . . with a sacramental spirit.

We live and act, based on our current strengths. The **Twelve Keys** are listed in their order of importance, value, and priority. We do not act on them in that order. For example, one, helpful, legendary, mission outreach is first in order of importance, value, and priority among the **Twelve Keys.** It is the passion of my own heart.

Rarely is mission outreach the first key on which we act.

We grow forward where we *can* grow forward, not where we think we *should*. We build on what we do well. We might expand a current strength in shepherding visitation and add a new strength in significant relational groupings. We might expand a current strength in stirring, helpful worship and add a new strength in adequate parking.

Over time, we may work our way to mission outreach. The first key—mission outreach—is like playing pro ball. We play junior high ball, high school ball, and college ball before we head to pro ball. Some of the other keys are less complex than the first one, mission outreach. *We do well what we do well and learn as we grow forward.*

A few congregations leap eagerly to the first key, mission, before they have achieved real strength in some of the other keys. They try to play pro ball, not having learned how to play junior high or high school ball. They try to sing a complex piece of oratorio music before they have learned how to sing a simple melody. They get burned.

Regrettably, they back off from mission. Having gotten burned, they do not get near mission outreach for years. The art is to grow forward where we can grow forward. The art of living is to build on the current strengths with which God blesses us. The art of action in a congregation is to do the same. We live and act on the strengths God now gives us.

We may deliver strengths of shepherding, worship, groupings, leaders, and decision making, these five relational strengths, so well that mission outreach, the first central characteristic, comes along. Feel free to focus on what you can do, among the **Twelve Keys.** Do not get caught up in doing them in the order they are on the chart.

Our living and our action build on the current strengths with which God blesses us.

Strong, healthy congregations share these basic qualities: grace, strengths, compassion, excellent sprinters, and act swiftly. We share these basic qualities, as we grow forward some of the **Twelve Keys** to which God invites us. We sense God encouraging us to expand this current strength, to add this new strength. We act swiftly. We live in the grace of God.

Part Two

THE TWELVE KEYS

ONE MISSION
OUTREACH

I was helping one congregation. We were in their sanctuary, praying and puzzling for the future of their congregation. One of the best things we do as Christians is pray. They had had thirty-seven losing seasons. We needed to gather all the prayer we could.

In the center wall of the chancel they have a remarkable stained glass window of Christ standing at the door, knocking. You remember the picture, the window, the Biblical image. In the long, lost churched culture of an earlier time, the understanding of the window was, "Christ stands at the door, knocking, hoping someone will hear the knock, and come to the door, and open the door and invite Christ **in** to their lives."

And, much was made of the fact that there was no doorknob or latchstring or keyhole on the outside of the door. We would be the ones who would hear the knock and we would come to the door and we would open the door and we would invite Christ **in** to our lives.

It dawned on me that day as we were kneeling at the altar rail, praying, with the sunlight streaming through the stained glass window in a remarkable way, what the picture, the window, the Biblical image means in our time: "Christ stands at the door, knocking, hoping someone will hear the knock, and come to the door, and open the door so Christ can invite them **out** into his life in mission."

Good friends, it is no longer that we invite Christ **in** to our lives. Now, Christ invites us **out into His life.** Where is Christ? In mission. Where does Christ live and die and is risen again and again? Among the human hurts and hopes God has planted all around us. Christ is in the world. When we are in the world, we are with Christ. It is not that we discover Christ, then go and serve in mission. It is in the sharing of mission that we discover Christ. In this new day, Christ invites us **out** . . . . to live and serve with him in mission.

One key, one possibility, for a strong, healthy congregation is one mission outreach.

A strong, healthy congregation:

- Shares *one* major mission outreach in the community
- Helps *directly* with one of these: a life stage, a human hurt and hope, a common interest, or a community concern
- Delivers concrete, effective *help* with persons and groupings *in the community*
- Is well known and well respected as *legend* in the community

Mission outreach is a gift of grace in people's lives and destinies. It is a gift freely given. We share mission outreach because God invites us to share a gift of grace. We will make a clearer distinction between mission and program, when we come to the chapter on program. For now, know that mission seeks to serve the community, and program seeks to serve the congregation.

ONE

People are grateful to discover a congregation who is a living presence of grace and mission . . . . who is sharing one mission

outreach in the community. People have the sense that this
congregation is among the giving and serving congregations of
the community . . . . living beyond themselves to share mission
outreach.

Many congregations have one, *major* mission outreach. At a
university or college, people have a major. Occasionally, some may
have a double major. They also have a minor, required courses,
and electives. People who have triple and quadruple majors tend
not to graduate. Congregations may do several mission outreaches. Strong, healthy congregations deliver one that is *major*.

Some congregations have none. They are preoccupied with
matters inside their congregations. They give only tangential
interest to the community and the world. Their focus is on
developing programs and activities inside their churches. They
huddle up inside. They hardly see their community around
them. They miss the world altogether.

Many congregations, by contrast, are strong and healthy
because they share one, helpful, legendary mission. Their longings . . . . yearnings . . . . their searchings are for mission growth.
They live out their longings by having *one* major mission outreach in the community.

The focus of their one major mission outreach is to serve
persons and groupings in the community. Some congregations
live out their one major mission by serving persons and groupings somewhere across the planet. Healthy congregations may
share their one mission outreach in the community and across
the world.

The church that tries to help everybody with everything
ends up helping nobody with nothing. It creates the mediocre
middle across the board. Strong, healthy congregations focus on
what they do well. When someone comes to them for assis-
tance with some concern that is not part of their major mission, they wisely refer the person to those who do well that
with which the person needs help.

One major mission outreach is sufficient in the hearts and
minds of a community. Community persons are grateful to

discover a congregation with a major mission outreach in the community. The result of this one mission outreach is that the congregation teaches the community it is a congregation of grace, compassion, community, and hope. It is a mission congregation.

POSSIBILITIES

Our one major mission outreach helps directly with a human hurt and hope, a life stage, a common interest, or a community concern.

God gives us many possibilities for mission. God touches us with signs of grace . . . . with areas of grace in our lives. Where grace touches our lives, there we discover possibilities for mission outreach. Indeed, grace touches our lives, now here, now there, so we will see these possibilities for mission.

We share the gift of mission outreach with a:

> human hurt and hope
> life stage
> common interest
> community concern

We may share a mission that is a combination of two or more of these four.

Human Hurts and Hopes. Grace touches our lives as we experience and live through human hurts and hopes.

The driver of the truck, weeping and crying, lamented that he could not stop in time. The young girl had dashed, suddenly, unexpectedly, quickly between two parked cars into the road. He slammed on the brakes, hard, harder, with all his strength. Squealing. Screeching. Not in time.

The young girl's death stirred three women in a congregation. They founded an after-school mission outreach to serve the life stage of early elementary children. Time has passed. Girls and boys are safe. They grow and develop in the after-school mission. It is the legendary mission outreach in the community.

Two men, in Akron, Ohio, discover one another . . . . their common longings . . . . their matching competencies. They launch a grouping to help persons wrestling with alcoholism. The AA movement was born to help with a specific human hurt and hope. Countless congregations are legends for their major mission outreach with AA in their own communities.

Here are some of the ways strong, healthy congregations live out their mission outreach with a human hurt and hope in the community:

Tragic events	Addictions
Grieving and leaving	Serious illnesses
Sinful events	Birthdays, anniversaries
Moving in to town	Graduations, special
Moving on to another town	celebrations
	Passing on, dying

There are many more. The art is to discover one human hurt and hope that stirs your passion and compassion.

Life Stages. Grace touches our lives as we transition from one life stage to the next.

Anticipation and expectancy are present at the beginning of each life stage. So are anxiety and fear. The art is sharing handles of help and hope that help persons through each stage of life.

Three women discovered their joy and love for preschool children. They found one another. They launched the legendary preschool in the community. Years later, I did a series of interviews with persons in the community. I would ask, "In addition to your parents, who meant the most to you in your growing up years?" Most persons gave the names of the three women.

They had been in preschool with them. Their preschool is the legend in the community.

Two persons became interested in helping senior adults in their community. They developed a seasonal grouping. There are three gatherings a year: fall, spring, and summer. The grouping reaches vast numbers of senior adults in the community. Solid help is shared. Many senior adults are helped.

Here are some of the ways strong, healthy congregations live out their mission outreach with a life stage in the community:

Birth

Infant

Preschool

Kindergarten

Early elementary

Late elementary

Middle school

High school

College, university, service,
    trade school

Early married

Early married with children

Vocation developing, changing

Open horizons

First grandchild

Caring for parents

Pre-retirement

Early retirement

Middle retirement

Late retirement

Pre older adult

Early older adult

Older adult

Fragile older adult

Multiple generations
    living together

There are many more life stages. Some persons in a congregation discover their longings to help with one life stage. The art is to discover one life stage that stirs your passion and compassion.

Common Interests. Grace touches our lives as we share a common interest.

Four women loved quilting. They were active in the same congregation. They shared ideas with one another: quilt designs, patterns, insights, and quilt blocks from their fabric stashes.

They decided, on behalf of their congregation, to do a quilting retreat one fall. They invited their friends. Word spread. Many people in the community came. The retreat was very successful. They were encouraged to have a spring retreat. They did. This retreat was even more successful.

In the time come and gone, the fall and spring retreats have reached many persons. Shepherding is shared. A sense of community is shared. Much more happens at a quilting retreat than quilting. The seasonal retreats have become helpful mission outreaches in people's lives and destinies.

Two families loved camping. Each summer they would camp together in the mountains of Colorado. They had great fun. Their families grew closer together, to the beauty of God's creation, and to the love of Christ. One summer, it came to them. They began a wonderful mission to help teenagers discover the beauty of God's creation and to discover Christ in a one-week camping event in the mountains of Colorado. Countless congregations are legends for their mission outreach with youth through this common interest in camping.

People discover one another as they share a common interest. They help persons live whole, healthy lives together, encouraging and shepherding with one another. These are some of the common interests with which congregations have shared in mission outreach with the community.

Flower gardening	Astronomy, stars
Quilting	Reading
Birds	Theater
Sewing	Shopping
Camping	Cooking
Chess	Woodworking
Bridge	Conversations
Games	Get-togethers

You will think of many more. The longing is to discover some common interest that draws us together as friends and family . . . . that helps us to discover roots, place, and belonging. The common interest helps us to fulfill our longing for community.

Concerns of the Community. Grace comes to us in the concerns of the community.

In a happenstance conversation after an education board meeting, five persons in a given congregation were visiting with one another. They had learned in the meeting that a very high percentage of youth never graduate from the local high school. They discovered their matching competencies. They launched a community-wide effort to improve the high school.

Their passion, competencies, and action plan carried the day. Some students still do not graduate from high school, but the percentage that do is now very high. Their congregation is a legend: "That's the congregation that loves youth." Many congregations are legends for their mission outreach in any one of the areas of community life.

Safety	Political
Education	Social
Poverty	Economic
Disease	Health care
Neighborhood, town	Energy
Region	Environment
Nation	Freedom
World	New discoveries

There are vast possibilities for grace, and, therefore, vast possibilities for mission outreach. The art is to deliver one of these as a major mission outreach in your community.

People discover a major mission outreach in a variety of ways:

Some persons discover something they have fun doing. They do it well. They share this as their mission outreach.

Some persons in a congregation "stumble" onto their one major mission outreach.

Some discover their longings to help with a human hurt and hope. They share concrete, effective help.

Some persons discover a congregation in their community that is sharing a legendary mission outreach. This mission stirs their compassion.

A precipitating event stirs some persons to discover their longings and competencies. They find one another. They launch one excellent mission outreach.

God comes to us in all of these ways to stir our passion and compassion to share in mission.

Frequently, the sequence is like this:

A precipitating event happens.

Three to five to eight persons find one another.

They discover their common longings.

They discover their matching, complementary competencies.

They launch a compelling mission outreach.

They deliver concrete, effective help.

The three to five to eight become fifteen and twenty . . . .

The mission becomes a legend on the community grapevine.

Time passes.

They turn around one year to discover they and their mission are legendary.

They did the mission for the sake of the mission, with deep humility.

This is why they are a legend.

I invite you to discover something you have fun doing. Look in your heart. Look around your community. Discover a congregation that is sharing well one mission outreach. Discover another congregation. Learn from them. Visit with your friends. Discover a common longing. Listen for a precipitating event that stirs your searchings and your strengths.

Our gift of a specific mission outreach is a gift of grace. As a congregation shares one, major mission outreach, the congregation shares grace, compassion, community, and hope. We live beyond ourselves. Our congregation is strong and healthy, effective and successful in sharing the grace of God.

HELP

Our one major mission outreach delivers concrete, effective help with persons and groupings in the community.

In an earlier time, we understood mission as sending money overseas, or sending money to some worthwhile project at home. Many congregations still do this. They do it well, with deep generosity. In this sense, money is mission. The congregation sends its money to the denomination. The denomination sends the money on. People receive the money. This is "third party" helping. God blesses the financial generosity of these congregations.

In our time, a major mission outreach includes persons in the congregation and persons in the community sharing their gifts, strengths, and competencies in "hands-on" ways. They share direct help with a human hurt and hope, a life stage, a common interest, or a community concern. This is "first party" help.

People long for some mission where they can be directly involved. They are happy to give generous money. What they want to do is give generous, direct help. They want to participate in sharing specific, concrete help. They want to share more than good intentions, glowing generalities, and syrupy sentimentalities. They want their help to be genuinely helpful.

The art of helping is to share just enough help to be helpful. In the parable of the Samaritan and the innkeeper, this is what happens. The Samaritan delivers just enough help to get the man, beaten and robbed, to the inn. The innkeeper delivers just enough help that the man, now restored, can be on his journey. The art of helping is to share just enough help to be helpful but not so much help that the help becomes harmful and creates a pattern of dependency and co-dependency.

The Samaritan did not go back to the place in the road where the man was beaten and robbed and set up a booth to help all persons beaten and robbed for the years to come. The innkeeper did not lavish so much help on the man that, out of gratitude and gratefulness, the man lived, lo, the rest of his days with the innkeeper. Sometimes, the grace of God comes to us as Samaritan, as innkeeper, to share just enough help that we can be on the journey of this life.

Many strong, healthy congregations share their mission outreach in one-time, seasonal, short-term forms of mission. Some congregations share their mission outreach in long-term and weekly, monthly, year-round ways. God blesses all of these forms of mission. God especially blesses the congregations who give just enough help to be helpful but not so much help that patterns of dependency and co-dependency are created. The key is to deliver concrete, effective help. It is not how often we help. It is not the frequency of the help. The key is that the help helps.

Strong, healthy congregations share their mission outreach with the motivations of compassion, community, and hope. God blesses us with these motivational resources to lead us to mission outreach. Mission is compassion. Compassion is mission. Mission is community. Community is mission. Hope is mission. Mission is hope.

Compassion casting is more helpful than vision casting. Community casting is more helpful. Hope casting is more helpful. Vision casting resonates with persons for whom challenge is their primary motivation. More people motivate themselves to mission out of compassion, community, and hope than out of challenge.

Compassion casting resonates with persons for whom compassion is their primary motivation. We share a mission with a spirit of compassion. This resonates with the compassion in the persons with whom we are in mission. Both the persons sharing the mission and the persons benefiting from the mission discover one another in their compassion, community, and hope.

LEGENDARY

Our one major mission outreach is well known and well respected as a legend in the community.

Think of persons in your community. When the name of your church is spoken with them, what comes to their minds? If it is a committee meeting and a line-item budget, we are in trouble. If it is a location and a building, we are a little better off. Mostly, we have this mission strength well in place when people say, "Oh, that is the congregation who loves children."

In many villages, towns, and cities, I will share the name of a given congregation. People say,

"Oh, that is the congregation who helps the poor."
"Oh, that is the congregation who loves alcoholics."
"Oh, that is the congregation who loves the elderly."
"Oh, that is the congregation who loves sports kids."
"Oh, that is the congregation who is helping the schools."

They will name a human hurt and hope, a life stage, a common interest, or a community concern.

All these persons teach me that they think of some specific mission outreach when they think of these congregations. These are congregations who share one helpful mission in the community. They have become legends for this one mission outreach with persons who live in the community.

In a community there are a range of groupings:

persons who participate in this congregation
persons who are active in other churches
persons who live in the community and think well of this
    congregation
community persons who do not participate in any church

Most of these persons do not know the statistics that show the amount of money a congregation gives away to support various mission projects, here and abroad. What they do know is what the community grapevine teaches them about what a congregation is doing, personally and hands-on, directly, with a specific mission outreach.

What they do know is that the mission serves directly persons and groupings in the community.

Many volunteers come from both the community and the congregation. The places of the mission happen in the community as well as the church. The resources and funding come from the generosity of both the community and the congregation.

What people do know is what they hear on the community grapevine. What they hear is of the children, who are loved, or of the poor, who are helped, or of the alcoholics, who are recovering, or of the sports kids who have found home, or of the schools, who have advanced.

Congregations become known on the community grapevine. Some are known for being warm and welcoming. Some for being helpful and serving in mission. Some for being cold and closed. Some for being preoccupied with themselves. What a congregation does or does not do teaches the community grapevine who the congregation is.

The mission is the deed of the creed. Strengths and mission are good friends. Our strengths lead us to mission. Mission helps us to claim our strengths. Twelve qualities help us live a healthy, generous, serving life. **Twelve Keys for Living** shares resources for developing these.

Discover two to three persons who share common longings and matching strengths for mission. Deliver concrete, effective help. Share the mission for the sake of the mission. The two, three become eight, twelve, twenty. Some helped in the mission become helpers in the mission. Some community persons decide they want to be part of the mission. The mission becomes a legend on the community grapevine.

We share in mission. A melody moves in us, a harmony lifts our lives, a singing stirs us. We hear the music of life, fully, clearly. We are at one with the universe. The grace of God is close. Mission stirs our souls, encourages our hearts, and leads us to our best true selves. We sing the grace of God. We have this confidence . . . . this assurance. God gives us strengths sufficient unto the mission with which God blesses us. We lead with the strengths God gives us.

Legendary congregations are a legend, not because they have tried to be, but because they have shared one, helpful mission in the community. They do the mission for the sake of the mission. They do not do the mission outreach for the sake of becoming known. The two by-products are: they become known (1) for their effective, serving help, and (2) for their humility of spirit.

A few people, or several people, or many people in a congregation share one, major, helpful mission outreach. Not everyone in a congregation participates in the one mission outreach. The Biblical principle is that there is a diversity of gifts. Not everyone has gifts, strengths, and competencies to share, effectively and helpfully, in a specific mission. Some people do. They have an abiding passion and excellent strengths to deliver a concrete mission. For the work of these few persons, the congregation, as a whole, becomes a legend on the community grapevine.

The mission outreach team has deep humility. They do not advertise. They do not boast of their work. Quietly and simply, they go about their mission outreach. The community grapevine does its work. The mission outreach becomes well known and well respected in the community. It becomes a legend.

We are not a legend because we think we are doing good work. We do not compare ourselves to others and conclude we are doing better work. We do not think this way. We focus our compassion, our passion, on the persons we are serving. We deliver concrete, effective help. We are grateful for the grace of God in our lives. We have humility before God's grace.

The community grapevine creates the legend.

Rating Guide: One Mission Outreach

Item	Maximum Points	Our Congregation's Rating
1. We have *one* major mission outreach in the community.	25	____
2. Our one major mission outreach helps directly with one of these: a life stage, a human hurt and hope, a common interest, or a community concern.	25	____
3. Our one major mission outreach delivers concrete, effective *help* with persons and groupings in the community.	25	____
4. Our one major mission outreach is well known and well respected as *legend* in the community.	25	____
Total	100	____

Instructions

- Use the resources of this chapter to evaluate your congregation's rating in each of the listed items.
- Enter your rating numbers in the blanks.
  Then, find the total.
- Divide the total of your score by 10 to obtain your congregation's rating on a scale of 1 to 10.
- Enter your rating of One Mission Outreach on the chart in Appendix C on page 258.

Further Resources

The Future That Has Come
Building for Effective Mission
Twelve Keys for Living
The Twelve Keys Bible Study

SHEPHERDING VISITATION

"I'm Bob Taylor. I've come to welcome you to our church family." He was standing on our front porch, tall, slender, graying hair, with a gentle smile. His words were grace.

We had moved into the rental house on Friday. That night, we discovered the other occupants of the house. The landlord had failed to mention the company. Three major nests of roaches. We spent most of Saturday battling the fray. We made solid headway. We were exhausted.

We decided we would go to church on Sunday morning. We made it on time. The service was helpful. We headed back to our rental house, changed clothes, continued to unpack, and to do battle with the unwelcome, hopefully, soon to be gone, former residents.

The air conditioning was on the blink. It was a hot, humid August day. We were not having fun.

Bob Taylor was the senior pastor of the church. We were amazed to see him standing on the porch. We had been to the church that one time. We invited him in. We shared a pleasant, brief visit. I do not remember much of what he said. The fact that he came was grace enough. I do remember that his interest was in us. He inquired of our lives. He shared a gentle, shepherding spirit with us.

In the years come and gone, that we were active in that church, we did much of all that we did in grateful appreciation for Bob Taylor's shepherding visit. His visit "restored" our souls.

One key, one possibility, for a strong, healthy congregation is shepherding visitation.

Shepherding is an art we grow forward. We learn it best when we live with a shepherding spirit in day-to-day life, when we do it regularly, with many persons, over a period of time. It is not an art one learns quickly or easily. It is the art of shepherding with people, discerning the times and ways that will share grace for this moment.

A strong, healthy congregation:

- Shares immediate, generous shepherding visits with persons who are in hospitals, homebound, in independent living, assisted living, and nursing homes
- Shares generous shepherding visits with our congregation: members, constituents, and family and friends of our congregation
- Shares generous shepherding visits with our community: first-time worshipers, newcomers, and friends in the community
- Shares shepherding visits that have a sacramental quality that benefits and blesses people's lives

Shepherding is a spirit of loving, listening, learning, and blessing. People shepherd the way they experience being shepherded. When we shepherd, we share a word of grace that encourages a person in his or her own life. Shepherding is not primarily advising or coaching. These help persons discover an insight, a step, or an idea. Shepherding is restoring . . . . shares grace. It is a gift freely given. We do it because God shepherds us and invites us to share the blessing of shepherding with persons God gives us.

IMMEDIATE PERSONS

Our congregation shares immediate, generous shepherding visits with persons in hospitals, homebound, in independent living, assisted living, and nursing homes.

Hospitals. Our congregation is both generous and immediate with our shepherding visits with persons in hospitals and with their family and friends. We realize that one day in a hospital is like a week. It is not that time drags slowly by. Sometimes, it does. It is more like so many things happen so swiftly in one day in a hospital that it feels like a week of events has happened.

Gifted volunteers, our pastor(s), and our staff share these shepherding visits. They have gifts of grace and compassion, wisdom and encouragement. They have a sense of how long to stay and how to help the person, their family, and their friends. They have a spirit of gentle immediacy. They bless the person and their family.

Homebound. Many persons choose to live at home, even as they are no longer able "to get out and about" as they used to do. Their home is familiar. They manage pretty well. We generously visit with them, especially near significant events in their lives. Just because we know they are always there does not mean we "put off" visiting them. We visit regularly in our shepherding visits with them. We develop a pace of shepherding that is encouraging with them.

Independent Living, Assisted Living. Many persons, in this time, are finding their way to independent living possibilities.

Persons have left their own homes or apartments, mostly "down sized," and now live with a range of "close" neighbors in a group environment. Many are benefiting from assisted living. Many begin in independent living and, as time passes, move to assisted living. Our congregation is generous with our shepherding visits.

We share the gift of shepherding through the seasons of transition and settling that happen in the early days of the move. We shepherd during times of significant events, both past and present, in persons' lives. We help celebrate birthdays, anniversaries, events of loss, and special times. We are family with them, with a thoughtful, shepherding spirit.

Nursing Homes. Sometimes, persons in nursing homes are forgotten. They experience an occasional visit. Strong, healthy congregations are generous in shepherding with the person in a nursing home, the staff of the home, and the family of the person. Falls happen. Accidents occur. Illness overtakes us. Sickness comes upon us. We are immediate and generous in these times. We are present regularly.

On the community grapevine, our congregation is known for our spirit of compassion and shepherding with persons, family, and friends, especially with persons in hospitals, homebound, independent living, assisted living, and nursing homes. We are generous and immediate. If we could do one area of shepherding well, we would do this area very well. We are generous and immediate.

CONGREGATION

We share generous shepherding visits with our congregation: members, constituents, and friends of the congregation who live elsewhere.

Family. The family of our congregation includes both formal and informal members of our congregation. Constituents consider themselves informal members of the congregation. They participate in worship, some program, or some groupings. Theirs is a membership by participation.

Family and friends of our congregation often see themselves as part of our extended congregational family. They have family and friends with us. Their hearts are frequently with us. We shepherd with them in helpful and appropriate ways.

We share generous shepherding visits with our whole congregation. These visits are active—even proactive. They are not simply reactive. Yes, we share a shepherding visit in response to a family crisis or tragedy. We also share shepherding visits in day-to-day life. We do this for three reasons. First, we are building relationships, not simply waiting on events. Second, many times things have happened in a family that we do not know until we share a shepherding visit.

Third, our shepherding in times of everyday, ordinary life, with celebrative events, and with hope-fulfilling events makes it deeply possible for us to shepherd in tough, tragic times. We come, not as a stranger, but as family.

Our shepherding visits are generous, frequent, and active. Our visits are not reluctant, occasional, and reactive. The grace of God is generous, frequent, and active with us. We visit generously because God generously visits with us. God restores our souls. We share the sacramental grace of shepherding visits because God does so with us. Our shepherding visits have a spirit of grace, humility, and compassion. We are not too busy to visit. We are generous with shepherding visits in people's lives.

We also encourage the informal shepherding groupings of our congregation. People are drawn to, participate in, and help to create informal shepherding groupings. Sharing and caring take place. Support and help happen. Good fun and good times occur.

We shepherd one another in everyday ordinary life . . . . in celebrative events . . . . in tough, tragic times . . . . in events of

deep hope and new life . . . . We develop our informal shepherding groupings around some of these possibilities:

Relational, friendship networks	Life stages
Vocational villages	Human hurt and hopes
Common interests	Congregation networks
Recreational interests	Geographical locations

A healthy congregation is a family, a gathering, a collection of
many informal shepherding groupings, developed and developing from many possibilities. These informal shepherding groupings are open and inclusive, warm and welcoming. They include
persons in the congregation and in the community. People live
much of their lives in their informal shepherding grouping. They
do this before and after Sunday School or worship, out on the
patio, over coffee. It is so obvious that often we fail to see it.

You are welcome to gather the shepherding leaders of your
current informal groupings. You are welcome to give them
these four sacramental gifts.

Share	give them the opportunity to share with one another, in a good fun, good times spirit of sharing and caring
Thank	thank them for their gifts of shepherding, share the gifts of *well done* and *thank you* with them
Encourage	encourage them with a spirit of confidence and assurance; share compassion, community, and hope with them
Bless	with a sacred, holy act of grace and prayer, bless them for the ways they help persons live whole, healthy lives in the grace of God

We share intentional shepherding visits. We have persons
who do these visits well. We have many informal shepherding

groupings. We encourage a culture of shepherding. It is who we are. It is what we do. It is how we live. We are, by our very nature and practice, a congregation who shepherds well. We are a healthy shepherding family. We visit, because God first visited us.

Visiting. We visit with persons the ways they visit with one another. Some people, in day-to-day life, visit with one another over breakfast, morning coffee, lunch, afternoon coffee, or a five o'clock, near where they work. Some do much of their visiting by phone. Some share personal notes by e-mail or mail. Some visit with text messages. Indeed, people share visits, stay in touch with one another, share shepherding, in our time, in a wide range of ways:

> personal visit at work
> personal visit at common interest, recreational, community gathering place
> personal visit at home
> small group gathering, large group gathering
> personal phone call
> personal note
> personal e-mail note, anecdotal interest e-mail
> personal text message note
> web site or blog
> social networking opportunities, such as Facebook or Twitter

Think of how the person "visits" in day-to-day life. You are welcome to visit with the person the way he or she visits with friends and family in everyday life. It is not the location of the visit, but the quality of the shepherding, that makes a visit helpful.

Seasons for Shepherding. We shepherd with a sense for the changing of the seasons of life. Every culture, every community, develops several seasons for the year. The transition from the ending of one season to the beginning of the coming season is an important time to share shepherding. During this transition time, anticipation, creativity, and hope can be at their highest. Likewise, anxiety levels, and therefore, potentially, fear and anger levels can be at their highest.

These seasons will vary in the United States, Australia, Canada, Korea, New Zealand, and beyond. In a senior adult culture, the seasons will vary. In your culture, the seasons will be distinct. Whatever the seasons, the key point is this: the anticipation and anxiety levels will have a rhythm of life that matches the local seasons of life. Shepherd well in these seasons of transition.

Ways and Times. We shepherd with one another in the rhythms of life. We do not shepherd only in tough, tragic times. Our shepherding in times of everyday ordinary life, with celebrative events, and with hope-fulfilling events makes it deeply possible for us to shepherd in tough, tragic times. We come, not as a stranger, but as family.

We share shepherding with one another in one or more of these ways. We do not try to be helpful in all seven of these ways in a single visit. Frequently, the gift we share is loving, or listening, or learning. Sometimes, the gift is celebrating, or encouraging, or coaching. With compassion and wisdom, we discern the gift helpful for the time.

	Times of Shepherding			
	Everyday, Ordinary Life	Celebrative Events	Tough, Tragic Times	Hope-Fulfilling Events
Ways of Shepherding				
Loving				
Listening				
Learning				
Leading				

Celebrating
Encouraging
Coaching

Everyday, Ordinary Life

> pleasant visits, coffee, car pooling, shopping, golf, recreation, sharing

Celebrative Events

> birthdays, anniversaries, special times

Tough, Tragic Times

> troubling events, accidents, sinful events, disasters, illness, passing on

Hope-Fulfilling Events

> events where our deepest yearnings and longings are fulfilled . . . . a wedding, a graduation, a new child, a close friendship discovered, a significant accomplishment achieved, an event of great grace, passing on

Shepherding is an art we grow forward. We learn it best when we live with a shepherding spirit in day-to-day life . . . . when we do it regularly . . . . with many persons . . . . over a period of time. It is not an art one learns quickly or easily. It is the art of shepherding with people, discerning the times and ways that will share grace for this moment.

COMMUNITY

Our congregation shares generous shepherding visits with our community: unchurched, newcomers, friends in the community.

Gifts. Our shepherding visits with community persons are our gifts with these persons and with the community as a whole.

There is a direct correlation. The stronger the shepherding in the community, the stronger the character and quality of life in the community. We want the community to be a strong, healthy community. Our shepherding visits in the community help decisively.

We share shepherding visits with a spirit of balance—visiting with the congregation and visiting with the community. We have "one foot in the church and one foot in the community." When the focus of shepherding is only within the church, one of the major sources of helping in the community is lost. When the shepherding is primarily in the community, the strength of sharing with those in the congregation is lost.

Many of our shepherding visits are informal. We visit with the groupings in the congregation and in the community. Shepherding takes place as we visit with quilting groups, football gatherings, music groups, and a range of congregation and community events. Some of our visits are formal, carefully organized, planned visits. We work out a time and place that works well for the persons we look forward to visiting and for our schedule.

Congregations are blessed with many persons who have shepherding gifts. Regrettably, some of them are serving on committees. Their best gifts are in shepherding. I encourage us to fill our shepherding teams before we fill our committees—to fill people's lives with shepherding visits. Our shepherding visits are shared by a range of our key leaders, grassroots, and pastor. We focus on people first, and programs second.

We share gifts of shepherding in the community that match the strengths with which God blesses us. We share these visits with "no strings attached." We have "no hooks." We simply share these visits as gifts of grace.

Persons. Our community includes unchurched persons who have lived in the community for some time, and do not actively participate in a congregation. Someone says to me, "Oh, well, we are Southern Baptist." I know immediately the likelihood is that they are unchurched. You will see it. A Southern Baptist, who is *active* in a congregation, will usually say, "We go to First Baptist. Brother Jimmy is our pastor."

When someone gives us the name of a denomination, whether it be Presbyterian, Methodist, Lutheran, mostly they are teaching us the church of their childhood memories or the church where they have an affiliation and are not active. The truth is that the largest denomination on the planet is the denomination of the unchurched. We share shepherding visits with unchurched persons God has given us in our community.

Our community includes newcomers to the community. True, in some communities, persons moved in thirty years ago, and they are still considered "newcomers." Here, I have more in mind persons and families who have moved in recently—in the immediate six months to a year. As best one can, it is helpful to visit with them soon after they move in.

Sometimes, moving is not all it is cut out to be. The job may not be quite what was promised. The neighborhood children may not have embraced the new kids. The house has its share of surprises. The welcoming visit of a shepherding person is a gift of grace. We are not "the welcome wagon" person who has information about shops and stores, coupons and directions.

We visit to share with them . . . . to bless them . . . . to bless their new home. We are intentional in *welcoming* them. We are not "trying to get them to come to church." We are *being the church with them in their new home.* We are developing a relationship of sharing and caring, serving and blessing.

Our community includes what I call "friends in the community." For example, the Salvation Army has many friends in the community. These persons are not members of the Army, nor do they participate in the Army. They think well of the Army and give generous support to the Army. From time to time, they help out with a project the Army is doing. They are friends.

Many congregations have persons in the community who are friends. They are not members. They are not participants.

For a worthwhile project, they help. They give generous support. They give time. They think well of the congregation and our mission. We share shepherding visits with them. We are not trying to get them to do more. We share grateful visits of appreciation.

In an earlier church culture, it was "the thing to do" to go to church. People sought the church out on their own initiative. We could get away with not doing much shepherding in the community. Not so in our time. But, do not mourn for that long lost church culture. The church is never at its best in a churched culture. The church becomes bloated and bureaucratic, lazy and indifferent. Too much, it enjoys the pedestal, prestige, and prerogatives of a churched culture.

The church is at its blazing best on a mission field. That is where the church was born. This is where the church is most at home.

SACRAMENT

Our shepherding visits have a sacramental quality that benefits and blesses people's lives.

The Spirit of Shepherding. We visit with the spirit of a good shepherd. Our text is:

> The Lord is my shepherd.
> I shall not want.
> He makes me to lie down in green pastures.
> He leads me by still waters
> He restores my soul . . . .
>
> PSALM 23:1–3A

A shepherding visit restores our souls. This is the spirit of shepherding.

A shepherd does not boast or boss. A shepherd does not bully and intimidate. A shepherd does not do co-dependent and dependent behavior. A shepherd does not dictate and dominate. A shepherd is gentle and kind, encouraging and generous, helpful and hopeful, with compassion and wisdom, integrity and honesty. A shepherd restores one's soul.

Life and Sacrament. Life is a pilgrimage. One of the rare gifts of our pilgrimage on this planet is the discovery of people with whom we can develop sharing and caring relationships. In shepherding visits, people seek out their fellow human beings and begin to develop the sense of common pilgrimage, one with another.

Shepherding is the creed in action.

Over the years, I have observed, "The more shepherding, the less bickering. The less shepherding, the more bickering." I help congregations who have neglected shepherding for ten or more years. When the shepherding stops, the bickering begins. The solution to bickering, fussing, feuding, and fighting is in shepherding. As we shepherd, we grow in the grace of God.

I have observed, "The more shepherding, the more worshiping. The more shepherding, the more volunteers. The more shepherding, the more giving." There is a direct correlation between shepherding, worshiping, volunteering, and giving. The more helpful the shepherding, the stronger the worship, volunteers, and giving—the stronger people grow forward in the grace of God. We share shepherding, finally, not to stop the bickering, increase worship, volunteers, and giving. These are happy by-products that emerge.

A visit is a sacrament.

This is why we visit. The purpose of our visit is sacramental. We are not visiting to hustle. We are not there to hawk neat, nifty programs and activities. We are not there to get and give information. Some people suggest there is no point in visiting. They say it does not grow a bigger church. The purpose of a sacramental visit is to grow persons, not churches . . . . to help persons to live a deeper, fuller life in the grace of God. The purpose is to bless persons.

Shepherding is a sacrament.

An act of shepherding is an act of grace, compassion, community, and hope. It is not just a thing we do; it is the way we love. Together, we discover compassion, sharing, and caring in our shepherding visit. We discover deeper, more profound relationships among friends, fellow voyagers, and family through this life's journey. In the act of shepherding, we experience the grace of God. We share compassion. We are community. We live in hope.

The visit is a sacred, holy act of grace.

We search for . . . . long for . . . . some gesture, some act, some visit, some sign, some spirit of compassion that touches our lives . . . . restores our sense of well-being . . . . helps us to feel whole once again. We yearn for forgiveness, reconciliation, moving forward. We long for compassion . . . . shepherding.

We search . . . .
　　　we search . . . .
　　　　　we search . . . . for compassion.
We discover the blessing of God's compassion.
　　　We cherish this sacramental gift.

Rating Guide: Shepherding Visitation

Item	Maximum Points	Our Congregation's Rating
1. Our congregation shares immediate, generous shepherding visits with persons in hospitals, homebound, independent living, assisted living, and nursing homes.	25	_____
2. We share generous shepherding visits with our congregation: members, constituents, and family and friends of our congregation.	25	_____
3. We share generous shepherding visits with our community: first-time worshipers, newcomers, friends in the community.	25	_____
4. Our shepherding visits have a sacramental quality benefiting and blessing people's lives.	25	_____
	_____	_____
Total	100	_____

Instructions

- Use the resources of this chapter to evaluate your congregation's rating in each of the listed items.
- Enter your rating numbers in the blanks. Then, find the total.
- Divide the total of your score by 10 to obtain your congregation's rating on a scale of 1 to 10.
- Enter your rating of Shepherding Visitation on the chart in Appendix C on page 258.

Further Resources

Visiting in an Age of Mission
A New Beginning for Pastors and Congregations
Small, Strong Congregations
The Twelve Keys Bible Study

3

STIRRING, HELPFUL WORSHIP

Richard said to me, "Dr. Callahan, we want you to know that the first Sunday we came, Mary so warmly welcomed us, we just knew we had found home.

"We had been to a couple of congregations. No one really spoke to us. Oh, in a perfunctory kind of way, they would say, 'Good morning' and hand us a bulletin. But, then, they would go back to talking among themselves. It was as if we did not exist. No, we would have been uncomfortable if everyone rushed over. That would have been overwhelming and intimidating.

"We were so glad Mary took a genuine interest in us . . . . as persons . . . . as family. This congregation is our family. And it began with Mary. We have found our years here most helpful."

One key, one possibility, for a strong, healthy congregation is stirring, helpful worship.

Through worship, people discover the grace of God in their lives. They discover their own strengths, gifts, competencies for life, or their mission, their calling. They hear—perhaps for the first time—God inviting them to be helpful with some specific concrete mission. They learn some possibility for renewing or restoring the whole of their life, or they find some emerging sense of hope.

A strong, healthy congregation:

- Shares worship that is warm, winsome, and welcoming
- Shares music that is inspiring and dynamic
- Shares preaching that is helpful and hopeful
- Shares worship that is stirring, with balance, power, and movement

Worship speaks the language of the people God has given you to serve in mission. If you are working with an athletic group, learn the language of the athletic group. The prayers will match. The hymns will strike a chord.

Worship remembers the motivations of the grassroots: compassion, community, and hope.

Worship acknowledges the future that has come. We live among excellent sprinters, in a time of stars and galaxies.

Worship is a gift of grace, with no strings attached. Worship has little to do with church growth. It has much to do with helping people grow lives of grace.

WARM

Our congregation shares worship that is warm, winsome, and welcoming.

The Congregation. The worship service is warm, winsome, and welcoming because the congregation is warm, winsome, and welcoming. We walk into some congregations and immediately feel the spirit of warmth and welcome that pervades the group. We feel at home. Parking greeters welcome us and help us find a place to park. Door greeters greet everyone—members, constituents, and visitors.

New-person greeters stand away from the door and seek to greet new persons. New-person greeters are warm, sincere, thoughtfully friendly individuals with a natural ability to help people to feel at home. People begin to think of the congregation as their home because people welcome them and care for them in simple ways.

Ushers have a sincere spirit of warmth and tenderness. They do not simply hand out bulletins or take up the offering. They help to seat new persons near someone who will help them feel at home. As people are seated and look around, they make some decision about whether this is home. People evaluate how well they fit in based on who they see sitting around them.

The entire progression—from the parking lot, to the narthex, to the pew—has a spirit of warmth about it. Parking greeters, new-person greeters, ushers, and persons in the congregation welcome us. Friendship, in beginning ways, has been experienced and expressed. Throughout this progression, first-time worshipers are greeted with love and warmth. They feel welcome. They have found a place where Christ's words of grace and community, hope and resurrection are real.

A further source of warmth and winsomeness is the leaders of the worship service. They share their sense of warmth implicitly and explicitly. The worship leaders convey a sense of grace, forgiveness, reconciliation, and hope. This has to do with the spirit in which the service is led more than it does with the order of service itself. The more the service is led out of a theology of grace, the more likely all persons experience the service as sharing warmth and winsomeness.

We are welcome as part of the family.

We walk into other groupings and sense a subdued, distant, chilly atmosphere. Some funeral services have a better spirit of celebration and joy. A few people talk to us. They are polite with us. There is distance. We are strangers. Visitors.

With warm, winsome congregations, we sense a warm, winsome, and welcoming spirit. When I interview persons and ask why they decided to make this their church home, most often, they say, "The first Sunday we came, John so warmly welcomed us, we just knew we had found home." The names change. The spirit is the same.

They do not say, "Everyone rushed over to greet us." That would be overwhelming and intimidating. They do have the sense they are part of the family because one or two persons helped them to feel at home. This is most important.

It is in the phrase, "We can never make a first impression a second time." Eighty percent of the decision as to whether first-time worshipers ever come back is made in their first worship experience with us. Do not believe the studies that say people visit eight, ten, or twelve times before they decide. Those studies are only done among the people who came back.

Before a worship service begins, some congregations look like they are having fun. There is a spirit of joy and celebration, anticipation and reverence. For other congregations, there is stilted silence. It is not reverence. It is coldness. Distance. It is as if these persons almost seem not to even like one another. You can feel it in the air.

With many congregations, there is a sense of gathering and enthusiasm. It feels like people want to be here. They long to share with one another. There are warm greetings and gentle hugs. There are smiles of gladness. People look happy. They feel happy. It feels like a wedding feast of God's grace. It feels like a great banquet of God's hope. It feels like home. We are warmly welcomed.

These congregations live a theology of grace. The sense of warmth and winsomeness grows out of their experiences with the grace of God. They share a theology of love . . . . a theology of community. They live as the body of Christ. They are family together, gathered in the grace of God, the compassion of Christ, and the hope of the Holy Spirit. They are a community . . . . a fellowship that shares grace, strengths, help, and hope.

Our Worship Home. The worship service is warm, winsome, and welcoming because the worship space is warm, winsome, and welcoming. Our worship space, our sanctuary, is warm and welcoming because of its

shape
colors, textures, and lighting
seating

Shape. The shape of most worship spaces is warm and welcoming. Simple rectangular spaces, square spaces, and circular spaces all tend to be inviting. Some spaces have an awkward confusion of circular and rectangular lines with elaborate ornamentation that tends to be off-putting with people. By the same token, some of the great cathedrals share a spirit of grace and welcomeness that people just know they have found home. With some spaces, many steps are foreboding. Tiny vestibules and narthexes tend to be unwelcoming. Narrow aisles and steep slopes are not helpful.

Colors, textures, lighting. Attractive, warm, light colors are more helpful than cold, dark colors. The textures of the floors, walls, ceiling, seating, and chancel are in harmony. They share a sense of unity and congruity, of warmth and of an inviting spirit. The lighting is pleasant and generous. Some of this is from natural lighting. In winter climates, we do not depend primarily on natural lighting. We have generous lighting for seeing, reading, and for sharing a sense of community with one another. The chancel area is well lit. The rubric is: the larger the space, the warmer the lighting. A well lighted sanctuary feels like home.

Seating. The impact of the worship space contributes to the sense of warm, winsome, and welcoming. We develop *perceptions* in response to the surroundings in which we share worship. Generally speaking, the experience of stirring, helpful worship takes place in comfortably filled worship seating.

There are these possibilities of worship seating:

	City	**Rural**
Uncomfortably crowded	Above 80%	Above 60%
Comfortably filled	80%	60%
Comfortably empty	60%	40%
Uncomfortably empty	40%	20%

In cities, worship spaces are comfortably filled at 80 percent of seating capacity. In town and country settings, the worship space is comfortably filled at 60 percent of seating capacity. People who have chosen elbow room in everyday life—living five to ten acres, or more, apart—want a similar sense of spaciousness in their worship space.

Several factors contribute to a worship space being in the comfortably filled seating range: a wide center aisle or aisles, wide side aisles, a large vestibule, comfortable chairs or short pews, and a spacious chancel at the front of the worship space.

Wide aisles contribute to the ease of entering and leaving the worship space. The roominess they provide allows freedom to stop and greet someone without obstructing others as they move to find their seats. The visiting and fellowship before and after the worship service enhances the sense of togetherness and community.

A large vestibule is a helpful gathering area for establishing relationships through visiting, sharing, and caring. Importantly, a large vestibule gives worshipers a strong first impression of openness and spaciousness.

Comfortable chairs provide a sense of individual seating, which many people welcome in our time. Individual chairs, when comfortable and well designed, help people sit closer without feeling uncomfortably crowded. People have the sense of their own individuated space. In cities, so long as the chairs are not placed too close to one another, people will not feel uncomfortably crowded until the sanctuary is 90 to 95 percent filled.

Short pews, seating up to eight people, are more desirable than longer pews. Many people arrive early in hopes of finding their aisle seat. Some people will step past those on the aisle to sit more toward the middle of a pew, but generally people don't like to feel "trapped" in the middle. Many people are particularly sensitive to seating that feels claustrophobic.

The chancel area delivers a sense of openness and spaciousness for the sanctuary as a whole. When people look forward, what they see shapes how they feel. The more spacious and open the chancel area is, the more likely people are to feel comfortable in their seating, even if they are, in fact, somewhat crowded.

Some chancels feel closed, cluttered and crowded. When people look forward to the chancel, they experience the closedness, clutteredness, and crowdedness. A worship space that is, in fact, comfortably filled, now feels uncomfortably crowded because of the crowdedness of the chancel. By the same token, an open, spacious chancel helps an uncomfortably crowded worship space feel comfortably filled.

People prefer a worship space that is comfortably filled. Next, people prefer comfortably empty. Then, people prefer uncomfortably empty. Last of all, people put up with uncomfortably crowded. They will do so mainly on Christmas Eve, Christmas, and Easter. These are very special events. From Sunday to Sunday, people prefer not to worship in a sanctuary that is uncomfortably crowded.

In Appendix B, you will discover Chart B.1, the maximum "comfortably filled" seating capacity formula to assess the seating range of your sanctuary.

A congregation with an *uncomfortably crowded* worship space is wise to accomplish one or more of these possibilities:

1. Deliver compassionate shepherding, inspiring music, helpful preaching, and adequate parking. With these four factors well in place, a congregation can sustain an uncomfortably crowded worship attendance Sunday after Sunday.
2. Deliver two of the first four keys—mission, shepherding, worship, groupings—with extraordinary excellence. We deliver *so well* two of the sources of satisfaction that people are at peace about the worship space being uncomfortably crowded. They are sharing worship with one of the legendary congregations in the community.
3. Add another service, or two new services, one soon, and one in a couple of years.
4. Expand the size of the sanctuary.
5. Consider building a new sanctuary.

Worship spaces tend to plateau at comfortably filled. They will push beyond that for a time. Then, they fall back toward comfortably filled. For some, this looks like worship attendance is declining. Actually, it is simply falling back to the "people level" with which most people are comfortable.

A congregation with an *uncomfortably empty* worship space is wise to:

1. Deliver compassionate shepherding, inspiring music, helpful preaching, and adequate parking. People will put up with an uncomfortably empty worship space more easily when there is adequate parking. With these worship factors well in place, a congregation will be at peace about an uncomfortably empty worship space.

2. Deliver two of the first four keys—mission, shepherding, worship, groupings—with extraordinary excellence. When two of the sources of satisfaction are well delivered, people will be at peace about the worship space being uncomfortably empty. They share worship with one of the legendary, helpful congregations in the community.

Our congregation is warm and welcoming. Our worship services are warm, winsome, and welcoming. Our worship space is warm and winsome. People feel at home.

MUSIC

Our music is inspiring and dynamic.

Music is 40 percent of the service of worship. On those Sundays when my own preaching is off, I count on the music to carry the service. Music is extraordinarily significant in creating a service that is stirring and helpful. A strong music program has four ingredients: match . . . . whole . . . . size . . . . growing.

Match
Whole
Size
Growing

Match. Our music matches with and stirs our congregation. For many worship services, the congregation is the choir. The congregation's singing is the primary source of music for the service. People resonate with one another as they sing the music of the faith. The hymn book or the projection screen where the Scriptures unfold before them in music is the Bible with which many people are most familiar. People sing their theology.

Many congregations now have two or three services of worship. Each service has its own integrity of music that matches with that specific congregation. The music for the 8:00 service matches with the people for whom that service is "home." The 9:30 service has its own distinctive music. The 11:00 service has its own vibrancy of music that matches with the people for whom this service is "home." Were we three congregations, in three distinct buildings, five miles from one another, we would deliver distinctive music teams to each service. We might even deliver distinctive bulletins.

We would not ask some of 11:00 music group to go over to the 8:00 service and "cover" the music. We honor the distinctive groupings of people who come to each service. Sometimes, we have a music leader who can discern the distinctions and develop "matching" music and music teams for each service. Most often, we have a distinctive music leader for each service. We achieve matching music with each congregation.

Whole. There is a wholeness to the music, the liturgy, and the preaching. We do not have three different, independent parts, simply taking turn, one after another, in the same space. Each service has a spirit of both planning and spontaneity. Each service has unity and direction.

The persons who lead music, who lead liturgy, and who preach have trust and respect with one another. They share an excellent quality of teamwork. They move with spontaneity as a team when the Spirit leads them in a new direction during the worship service. Improvisation and spontaneity build on the planning that has already occurred.

Size. The size of the music team matches the size of the space. In some worship services, we have a choir, an orchestra, an organist, and a pianist helping with the music of the service. In some services, we have a vocal group, a band, several soloists, and special instruments. Whatever configuration of vocal and instrumental groups, the key is to have groups that match the size of the space. Further, it helps for such groups to match the size of the congregation.

We think this through with respect to a piano or an organ. We want a piano or an organ that matches the cubic footage of the space. The same principle is true with regard to any musical grouping that is in the space. The music needs to "carry the space." This does not mean that a small choir needs to sing louder. It does mean that we create a choir or music group that has the ability to "hold its own" in the worship space.

Growing. We count on the quality and depth of the music to be growing. The work of the pianist, the organist, the choir director, and the choir itself is of high quality. The music is played and sung competently. The people who sing and play share their compassion and their competencies. Both are fully present.

Someone's compassion does not compensate for a lack of competence. Indeed, it is precisely their compassion that fuels their desire to be among the most competent music groups to the glory of God in the community that surrounds the church.

This means that the music teams—vocal and instrumental—have a longing and yearning for growing their musical competencies. They look back and can see the progress they have made in the recent three years. They look forward to the progress they will achieve in the coming three years. Their spirit of growing influences the congregation's spirit of growing. We draw closer to the grace of God.

HELPFUL

Our preaching is helpful and hopeful.

The Spirit of the Preacher. Shepherd preachers have a spirit of grace and compassion. They share wisdom, the Gospel, good news. They have a gentle humor, not loud and bombastic. Their spirit is one of integrity, confidence, and assurance. Who they are is as important as what they say.

Grace is stronger than law. Law is strong. Grace is stronger. Helpful preachers have this spirit. Their spirit is grace, not law. Some preachers have a tendency to forget these gifts of God. By their spirit, some preachers turn grace into law, good news into judgment, and love into legalism.

Some preachers share a sermon on compassion, but the spirit with which they preach is a spirit of displaced anger and condemning judgment. What they say and the spirit with which they say it are in different, remote parts of the galaxies.

A preacher with a spirit of grace preaches with this rubric: relax, have fun, enjoy life, live in the grace of God. A preacher with a spirit of law is tense, tight, nervous, anxious, trying too hard, and by trying too hard ends up being too hard on the congregation. There are too many rules and regulations, conditions and stipulations. With a spirit of grace, a preacher shares good news, encouragement, and compassion.

The Content of the Sermon. Grace, forgiveness, reconciliation, moving forward, hope, new life . . . . these are central themes of content. Judgment, sin, and law are part of the Christian life, part of the human tensions within us and among us. There is the tension .... the constant struggle between law and Gospel, demand and grace.

The preacher who dwells week after week on judgment, sin, and law is telling only part of the message. It is difficult enough to live through a week in a world full of confusion and violence, disappointment, and despair. It is more difficult to live through a week when the preaching that is shared is a manifestation of that same confusion, violence, disappointment, and despair.

People are helped when the preaching leads them to the spirit of reconciliation, wholeness, caring, and justice. These are the persistent themes in the Biblical message.

The helpful preachers of our time have a spirit of humility and a passion for the Gospel. The quality of their preaching is rooted in grace and compassion. The character of their preaching has sufficient backbone to share in genuinely helpful ways. These are the preachers who are the shepherds and prophets in our time. They are shepherds in their caring and sharing. They are prophets with their thoughtful critique that advances help and hope in our time.

Christians, both clergy and grassroots, can once again discover the ringing message of the New Testament. Good News. Hope is stronger than memory. The Open Tomb is stronger than the bloody cross. The Risen Lord is stronger than the dead Jesus. The grace of God sustains us, the compassion of Christ surrounds us, and the hope of the Holy Spirit leads us.

The Delivery of the Sermon. "Who you are speaks so strongly that I *can* hear what you say." I find my phrase more helpful. I think it was Emerson who said, "Who you are speaks so loudly that I *cannot* hear what you say." I like my way better. Likewise, I say, "Who you are and how you say it, together, speak so loudly that I *can* hear what you say."

Excellent delivery enhances the message. Poor delivery distracts from the message. It is not that the delivery is fancy and erudite, scintillating and sensational. It is that the delivery has a sense of confidence and assurance, excellent eye contact, helpful gestures, and a warm "connection" with the congregation.

The delivery may be "down to earth." It may not be "polished." The delivery is comfortable and respectful. It is comfortable, in that it matches with the person who is preaching. It does not feel out of character. It is respectful, in that the delivery shows respect for the congregation. Awkward delivery, hesitant delivery, stumbling delivery—these do not respect the congregation. We are wasting the congregation's time with such delivery.

We share the delivery with a spirit of natural grace, well prepared and well practiced. In so doing, we demonstrate our respect for the congregation . . . . our respect for the Gospel. We are not wasting their time. We have thought well about the sermon. We have practiced it well. We share a helpful, hopeful sermon.

STIRRING

Our service is stirring. It has balance, power and movement.

Balance. The service is stirring and helpful when it has a sense of balance. I was helping one congregation. The minister of music said to me, "Dr. Callahan, I have had more complaints about the music in the last six months than in all prior ten years." I took a piece of paper and drew this chart.

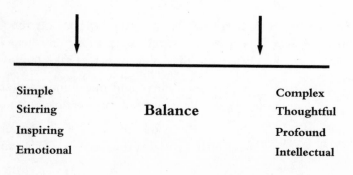

Simple	Complex
Stirring	**Balance**	Thoughtful
Inspiring	Profound
Emotional	Intellectual

I said to him, "We are emotional beings. We come to a service hoping some of our deepest longings and yearnings will be stirred and inspired. The service will touch our heart. We are intellectual beings. We yearn for our understandings of life to be thoughtfully and profoundly advanced. Teach me, eight of twelve Sundays where the preaching has been on this chart, and teach me where the music has been, during these past ten years." He knew immediately.

With considerable delight, he said, "Our prior pastor for ten years, before he retired, shared sermons that were toward simple, stirring, inspiring, emotional. The music, for the same ten years, tended toward complex, thoughtful, profound, intellectual."

"Yes," I said, "the service had a sense of balance. The music and the preaching mutually reinforced one another."

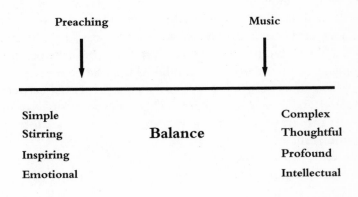

The pastor of ten years had retired. A new pastor had come, from a university community.

His sermons were long and complex. Multiple points. Lengthy parenthetical phrases. Fifty- and one-hundred-dollar words. "The eschatological significance of this soteriological text, in the light of the ecclesiology of the first century, has these onto-logical implications for our time." The people would say, "Amen." What else could they say?

They would leave the service feeling that the service did not feel quite like it used to. Surely, it could not be our learned new pastor with his impressive sayings. It must be the music.

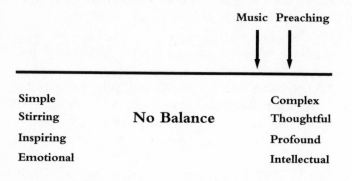

I said to the minister of music, "Good friend, from today forward, I count on the music, eight of twelve Sundays, to be toward simple, stirring, inspiring. We want to recover the balance of the service. Four of twelve of Sundays, be wherever you are drawn to be. For a variety of reasons, your new pastor is going to be toward complex and thoughtful every Sunday."

I went on to confirm, "This is not a trade-off between classical and pop Gospel music. There are countless classical pieces that are simple, stirring, inspiring. Beethoven's *Ode to Joy* is among them."

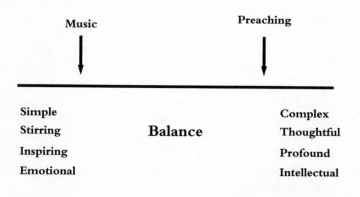

For congregations, the type of service is an important consideration. There are at least fourteen distinctive types of services that are being richly and fully shared somewhere on the planet.

TYPES OF WORSHIP

Traditional	Alternate
High Church	Jazz
Liturgical	Bluegrass
Gospel	Praise
Contemporary	Blended
Seeker	Generation
Family	Stadium

The balance of the service is as important, indeed, slightly more important. It is not so much that the words of the music reinforce the words of the message. It has more to do with the spirit of the music and the spirit of the preaching having some sense of balance with one another. Most people have not been to a seminar on the fourteen types of worship. What they intuitively know is that the service has a sense of balance . . . . or it does not.

A contemporary service with complex contemporary music and complex teaching preaching will feel out of balance. A high liturgical service with complex liturgical music and complex teaching preaching will feel out of balance. It is not the type of service. It is the balance of the service that helps.

When the pastor plans on a teaching sermon, the music is simple, stirring, inspiring. When the preaching is complex, comprehensive, and intellectual, the music is simple, stirring, and emotional. On a Sunday when the music seeks to be complex, thoughtful, and profound, the preaching is simple, stirring, inspiring. Having complex music and complex preaching Sunday upon Sunday is neither helpful to the balance of a service nor helpful to the attendance at worship.

On Easter, Christmas Eve, and Christmas, we want both the music and preaching to be slightly toward simple, stirring, inspiring. For our best services, we want to deliver warm, winsome, welcoming services that have a simple spirit of power and movement. We do not want to deliver advanced trigonometry or fifth-year Latin. (I do have five years of Latin in my background.) We share basic math and first-year Latin. We share the beginnings of the Gospel, with inviting grace and joy, wonder and new life. We share the whole Gospel with the whole person through the whole service. We share balance.

Power and Movement. The service is stirring when it has power and movement. The service has a warm, joyful spirit. It is not loud and noisy. New-person greeters, ushers, and pew greeters help us feel at home. We look forward. The choir or music team is smiling, as though the Resurrection has just happened. The worship leaders and the pastor have a spirit of confidence and assurance. They are glad to be here. It feels like a sacramental family reunion, where people experience the grace of God.

Some services are cold, dull, and dreary. There are no new-person greeters or pew greeters. The ushers are minimally polite, passing out bulletins, and taking up the offering. There is hardly any eye contact. There is a formal, almost noticed, perfunctory greeting. When we look forward to the choir, we see the twins, "Doom and Gloom," slumped, shoulder to shoulder, cobwebs growing between them. Over the proscenium arches of some chancels the words are clearly written, "Behold, all ye who enter here shall never smile again." The worship leaders and the pastor are tense, tight, nervous, and anxious, trying too hard to hit a home run on every pitch.

By contrast, the worship service has power and movement when:

> the first three minutes go well
> the last three minutes go well

there are warm moments in the service
people discover one step

The first three minutes go well. If one thing can go well, let it be the first three minutes. We can never make a first impression a second time. Start strong. Grow stronger. If your announcements are in the first three minutes, they are well done, warm and inviting, with full eye contact, not read. We do not do poorly read announcements, call a time out, and say now the service is starting. The service begins whenever someone begins doing something up front.

The last three minutes go well. If a second thing can go well in the service, let it be the last three minutes. We can never make a last impression a second time. They have gone. End once. End well. Quit before people are ready for you to quit. Quit while you are ahead. Some services end four times, I think once for each of the four Gospels. They are services searching for an ending. Begin strong. End strong.

There are warm moments in the service. If a third thing can go well in the service, let it be the warm moments of the service. Warm moments touch the heart, stir the mind, lift the soul. Warm moments include a favorite hymn, a baptism, a special scripture, a story, an anecdote, the sacrament of communion well done, or some special event.

People discover one step. If a fourth thing can go well in the service, let it be the concrete help people discover to live, this coming week, in the grace of God. People discover one clue, insight, action, or feeling they can practice in the coming week to live a whole, healthy life in the grace of God. If a fourth thing can go well in the service, let it be the concrete help people discover to live, this coming week, in the grace of God.

The spirit of the service is more helpful than the type of service. Many liturgical services are warm and inviting. Many contemporary services are stilted, stiff, dull, and dreary, with people pounding away on their guitars in a lifeless, looking at the ceiling, hardly there, detached way. Many liturgical services go through the motions as well. We have many discussions on the type of worship. We benefit from more discussions on the spirit of the service.

Worship services of all types can have a spirit of power and movement. These services are a unified whole. Each stage of the service builds toward and contributes to the next stage in the service. There is a sense of progression toward the climax of the service—being in the world in mission as God's people.

Whatever type of service, people experience power and movement when the pastor is a shepherd. Then, the worship service will be stirring and helpful. The order is (1) shepherd, and, then, (2) preacher. One is, first, a caring shepherd; then, one becomes a helpful preacher. Some try to be a preacher before they have become a shepherd. They have put their cart before their horse.

In their preaching, two pastors both rank at 7 on a scale of 1 to 10. One is a shepherd, as well as a preacher. The shepherd preacher will be perceived by the congregation as preaching at a level of a 9. The other pastor—not a shepherd—will be perceived as preaching at a level of 5. It is a whole lot more fun to be a 9 than a 5. It is in the shepherding, not the preaching.

The shepherd preacher, in caring, loving ways, knows the people as a good shepherd. The shepherd preacher is able to preach, richly and fully, to their human hurts and hopes in everyday, ordinary life. A pastor who has not taken the time to be a shepherd with them will not know their specific hurts and hopes. Such a pastor can only preach generalized, innocuous sermons.

Further, when the people know that the pastor knows them, cares for them, and loves them, they listen more fully and attentively. They lean forward. This is their beloved shepherd speaking directly to them. They listen to shepherd preachers who share the Gospel in their lives as well as in their words, in their mission as well as in their message.

Genuinely and prayerfully, joyously and thoughtfully, we share stirring, helpful worship to help people experience the grace of God. Worship is a gift of grace in the lives of persons.

We search for . . . . long for . . . . hope . . . . some hint, some clue, some insight for living a whole, healthy life in the week to come. We yearn for some confidence and assurance for the present, the immediate future, the distant future, and the next life future beyond the River, with God in the life to come. We share our gift of hope for the sake of hope.

Hope is mutual. Sometimes, we find the hope. Sometimes, hope finds us. Sometimes, we find the Open Tomb. Sometimes, the Risen Lord finds us.

We search . . . .
   we search . . . .
      we search . . . . for hope.

We look around one day and discover the blessing of God's hope. We cherish this sacramental gift.

Rating Guide: Stirring, Helpful Worship

Item	Maximum Points	Our Congregation's Rating
1. Our worship services are warm, winsome, and welcoming.	25	____
2. Our music is inspiring and dynamic.	25	____
3. The preaching is helpful and hopeful.	25	____
4. Our service is stirring. It has balance, power, and movement.	25	____
	____	____
Total	100	____

Instructions

- Use the resources of this chapter to evaluate your congregation's rating in each of the listed items.
- Enter your rating numbers in the blanks. Then, find the total.
- Divide the total of your score by 10 to obtain your congregation's rating on a scale of 1 to 10.
- Enter your rating of Stirring, Helpful Worship on the chart in Appendix C on page 258.

Further Resources

Dynamic Worship
Preaching Grace
Twelve Keys for Living
The Twelve Keys Bible Study

4

SIGNIFICANT RELATIONAL GROUPINGS

I learned later what William had said to Tom. I had seen them in conversation on the other side of the room. Then, as I looked back a few minutes later, I saw Tom going out the door, leaving the meeting.

William had been president of the group for some time. I guess, as I reflect on it, that for William, it had become "his" group. Initially, as I saw them visiting, I had thought how gracious it was for William to go out of his way to welcome Tom.

What he had said to Tom was, "This is not your group. You do not belong here. I wish you would leave before I start 'my' meeting." Some time before, William and Tom had disagreed over some matter. I am not sure either of them could remember what the issue was.

Somehow, it had stuck in William's craw. Tom was well respected in the community. He was "a big fish in a big pond." William was, in reality, "a little fish in a little pond." He was threatened by Tom's coming to the group. William wanted Tom to know this was a closed group. It was. Tom never came back.

I was helping a congregation in a small town, not quite a county seat. I was there on Sunday morning. The choir had about twelve to fourteen singers. They were all in their seventies or eighties. Save one. On the second row, where altos frequently sit, there was a young girl. Her choir robe did not hide her condition. She sang with a quiet radiance. She looked peaceful.

I learned of her after church.

Some months before, she had told her parents she was pregnant. Her boyfriend had persuaded her, one time. Her parents were horrified. To be pregnant and unmarried was taboo in this small town. To be pregnant, unmarried, and fifteen was worse than worse. Her parents threw her out.

Her aunt took her in . . . . for a time. After several weeks, the family pressure on her aunt caused her aunt to ask her to leave. For a few nights Kate had been sleeping in a small shed at the back of the lumberyard. The nights were getting cold. Cooler weather was on the way. She did not know where to turn. No one would have anything to do with her. Word had spread.

On Sunday morning, she found her way to a church. Not her own church, in which she had grown up. In that last fiery, eruptive conversation with her parents, she had been warned to never come to the "family" church. She was cut off.

She was drawn to a church. She stumbled into this church, not knowing anything about it. She had never been there before. She just could not go on any more.

This congregation was more conservative than her childhood church. Their theology was sterner. Their moral standards were higher. They were of "old stock." They lived mostly in a time that had come and gone. They were of the "old school."

They took her in.

As I write these four words, I marvel at the miracle of that morning. What moved Grandma Ida Mae to do so, even later, she could not say. As Kate came in the door, and timidly hesitated, Grandma Ida Mae got up from her pew, and, with a gentle hitch in her step, walked down the aisle to the door, put her arms around Kate, and said, "Welcome home, Kate."

Everyone in the congregation had known of Kate's plight. It was a small town. Many in the congregation knew her aunt, her parents, and her whole family. The normal thing would have been to ask her to leave, or, perhaps worse, to ignore her . . . . pretend she was not there.

Grandma Ida Mae would normally have chosen to politely ignore her through the service, and in the fellowship conversation time following. She could not put into words why she welcomed Kate. She did say that she was certain Kate was helping her as much as she was helping Kate.

That Sunday, Kate found a new family.

Grandma Ida Mae took Kate to live with her. Kate became the daughter of the congregation. In the months come and gone, as Kate neared her time, the spirit of compassion and the sense of community deepened in the congregation. Grandma Ida Mae describes it as "a time of grace."

One key, one possibility, for a strong, healthy congregation is significant relational groupings.

A strong, healthy congregation:

- Has groupings that are open, inclusive, warm, and welcoming
- Has a healthy balance of one-time, seasonal, short-term, long-term, and weekly, monthly, year-round groupings

- Encourages many new groupings
- Has groupings through which people discover a depth of sharing and caring

In some movements, the focus is primarily on groupings that have an overt religious or spiritual quality about them. There are *many* areas in which you could grow groupings, not one. It is the gift of grace that counts in the grouping.

OPEN

Most of our groupings are open, inclusive, warm, and welcoming.

Informal and Formal. Many groupings are informal groupings. Some groupings are formal groupings. Informal groupings do not have a formal meeting structure. They do not have formal rules and regulations, policies and procedures. They sort of, in a loose way, live life together. Informal groupings gather around:

> friendship and relational networks
> a life stage
> some human hurt and hope
> the same vocational village
> a common interest—recreational, intellectual, work project, social, music, art . . . .
> some community concern
> a combination of two or three of the above

Informal groupings have:

> goals and values
> customs, habits, and traditions
> a common language and communications network
> a leadership and decision process
> common patterns of behavior

sacred places of meeting
a common shared vision of the future

Formal groupings have these qualities as well. They also
have a formal meeting structure. They have formal policies and
procedures, rules and regulations. They have a formal agenda as
to what they are seeking to achieve.

In our time, many people are drawn to informal groupings.
People exercise considerable creativity, imagination, self-direction,
self-control, and energy to start, develop, and participate in
an informal grouping. The mistake some make is to focus on
developing only formal groupings. The art is to create both
informal and formal groupings. Many find home in an informal grouping. Some find home in a formal grouping.

Open, Not Closed. Both informal and formal groupings have
the possibility of being open or closed. Groupings tend to head
toward being open or being closed. My research and experience
teach me that many groupings choose to be open groupings.
Some groupings, for reasons we will discuss in a moment, choose
to be closed groupings

Many Groupings	Some Groupings
open	closed
inclusive	exclusive
warm	clannish
welcoming	cliquish

For the most part, many groupings have a gracious spirit.
An open grouping is:

Open: It has a healthy and happy spirit. The participants have
a relaxed, generous spirit with one another and with new
persons. Mostly, they have shared healthy events together,
and look forward to healthy events in the future.

Inclusive: The grouping is sufficiently stable and resilient about its own relationships that it can embrace a new person. The already healthy relationships are enhanced with the new person's presence.

Warm: The grouping has a generous, warm, and relaxed set of goals and values, customs, habits, and traditions, and common shared sense of the future. The grouping is warm and relaxed with persons who have a slightly distinct set of goals and values.

Welcoming: The grouping shares generous hospitality. It has a natural, gracious spirit of welcoming new persons in their first time with the grouping.

A few informal and formal groupings are closed, exclusive, clannish, and cliquish. A "closed" group becomes closed for one or more reasons:

The grouping has been scared, or scarred, or both scared and scarred. The group has "huddled up" to protect themselves from being scared or scarred yet another time.

The grouping is sufficiently fragile and tenuous about its own relationships with one another; it feels it cannot endure yet another person. The already fragile relationships would collapse under the weight. A clique is a group *insecure* in its relationships, not secure. The insecurity is what causes the group to exclude new persons.

The grouping is intent on a rather rigid set of goals and values, customs, habits, and traditions, and common shared sense of the future. This rigidity causes the group to be closed to persons who have a slightly distinct set of goals and values.

In encouraging current groupings and starting new groupings, informal or formal, the art is to help a grouping to head toward being open, inclusive, warm, and welcoming.

BALANCE

Most of our groupings are one-time, seasonal, and short term.

Recall that we live in a time of excellent sprinters. Excellent sprinters do one-time, seasonal, and short-term groupings well.

One-time groupings gather for a one-time, self-sufficient, self-contained gathering. A congregation had a one-time, special covered dish supper gathering. It was a wonderful evening. People laughed and carried on. They hugged and embraced. It was like a best family reunion. As people were gathering their things to leave, someone said, "This was great fun." The group responded, "Yes!" The person said, "Let's do it every week." The person who said it was a solid marathon runner. In our time, the way forward for the congregation is to have another one-time, special covered dish supper at some point in the future.

People respond well to one-time gatherings. People experience a sense of family and community. People share and hug. They laugh. They celebrate. A wedding. A baptism. An anniversary. A camping trip. A Bible study. A recreational event. We will share, yet again, in another one-time grouping. For the moment, we remember the grace and compassion, the community and hope we shared together in the recent one-time grouping.

Seasonal groupings are like Vacation Bible School, an annual music camp, an annual youth camp, or a one-week summer Bible study. Basketball teams, soccer teams, and baseball teams are seasonal groups. Advent and Lenten groupings are seasonal groupings.

A quilting group has a fall retreat. They gather as a seasonal grouping. More than quilting happens. They share. They encourage. They bless one another. They look forward to the next fall retreat. Another quilting group has a spring retreat. The same encouraging dynamics happen. A grouping gathers for a summer vacation together. They have been doing so for many years. They are a seasonal grouping.

There are e-mails, notes, and phone calls in between each seasonal gathering. There is no "press" to meet weekly. They have discovered this: *it is the depth of their caring, not the frequency of their meetings, that counts.*

Short-term groupings happen over three to five gatherings. It could be over three to five weeks or three to five months. Excellent sprinters do three to five. You've seen it happen. Some group gathers, intending to meet for more than five times. Around the third or fourth or fifth gathering, attendance begins to drop off. Excellent sprinters are teaching us that they have gotten out of the venture what, for now, they plan to get out of the venture.

Were we to announce that some venture is going to go six, seven, eight, nine, or ten gatherings, some excellent sprinters will not show up for the first gathering. We have invited them to a marathon run. What they do well is short-term, excellent sprints. They do three to five "sprints." They do not do six plus.

Marathoners say, "If they were really committed, they would come to all ten." Excellent sprinters *are* committed. They are committed to excellent sprints, not long-distance marathons. One of our friends wins marathons in this country. He and I were visiting. He shared with me that he does not run marathons. He runs mile one in a certain time. He runs a *new* mile one in a certain time. He runs a *new* mile one in a certain time. He puts back-to-back twenty-six excellent sprints. This is how he wins a marathon.

Translation. Excellent sprinters come to worship *"this"* Sunday. They will be in worship forty-eight out of fifty-two Sundays so long as we keep the focus on, "Look forward to *'this'* coming Sunday." The minute we turn the focus to, "Be sure to be in worship *'every'* Sunday," we have put a sign out front that says, "No Room in the Inn for Excellent Sprinters."

Long-term and weekly, monthly, year-round gatherings happen over an extended period of time. Mostly, solid marathon runners come to long-term and weekly, monthly, year-round groupings. Long-term groupings tend to be groupings that gather for six plus sessions. Marathon runners come. Were we to turn six sessions into five sessions, excellent sprinters would come. Were we to turn ten sessions into two five-time sessions, excellent sprinters would come.

A "small group" emphasis grew up in a churched culture, a marathon culture, and an institutional culture. It was invented by solid marathon runners. It thrived. It helped well. It did solid work. It continues to do solid work wherever there is a high density of solid marathon runners.

We now live in a mission culture, an excellent sprinter culture, and a movement culture. In our time, many groupings are invented by excellent sprinters, including grandparents. The groupings thrive. The groupings help. They do solid work. They serve well the people God now gives us to help with their lives in the grace of God.

This does not mean we abandon long-term and weekly, monthly, year-round gatherings. We serve solid marathon runners. It means we have a healthy "balance" of groupings. This does not mean an equal number. We achieve balance by actually "looking at" the people God gives us to serve. Look at the people. Then, encourage groupings that match with the people God gives you.

Regrettably, most formal groupings have come into being because a committee decided "such-and-such" a grouping would be helpful. The hook is . . . . most of the people on the committee are solid marathon runners. *It takes being a solid marathon runner to endure the committee meetings. Excellent sprinters are not there.* Thus, the committee plans mostly long-term and weekly, monthly, year-round groups.

You are welcome to create a spirit in your congregation that encourages persons to begin a grouping that will be helpful with them in their lives. Feel free to share with them the five possibilities available: one-time, seasonal, short term, long term, and weekly, monthly, and year round.

Do **not** teach them that one-time, seasonal, and short-term groupings are simply "bait." Do not teach them that excellent sprinter groupings "hook" them, but now they need to "move along," that they will *really* be Christian when they are in a long-term or weekly, monthly, year-round grouping. That is the view of a solid marathon runner.

People grow forward in more than one way. Some people grow forward in solid marathon runner ways. Some people, many in our time, grow forward in excellent sprinter ways. Many people grow forward in both ways. No one way is better than the other. The art is to make available a range of ways. Encourage people to select the ways that are helpful with them.

Strong, healthy congregations have a healthy balance of one-time, seasonal, short-term, long-term, and weekly, monthly, year-round groupings. A grouping is a grouping because of the depth of its relationships, not the frequency of its meetings. Some say, "The only way you can be a group is to meet weekly or monthly." Some groups meet weekly or monthly and do damage and harm to one another weekly or monthly.

Each gathering of an AA grouping is a one-time gathering. In AA, people do not give up drinking forever, or even weekly or monthly. AA persons give up drinking "one day at a time." When an AA grouping gathers, it is a one-time gathering. The "lesson" for the gathering is a one-time lesson. The gathering has the spirit of self-sufficient, stand-alone, help for this one day.

Habitat for Humanity gathers people in a one-time grouping to build a one-time project: a specific house. There are a number of "get-togethers" as we build this one house. People sign up to build this one house. No one signs up to build a house *every* year.

Many persons grew up in marathon culture, and learned how to be solid marathon runners. Then, they had the fun of grandchildren. *They learned how to be excellent sprinters*. They retired and moved to Florida, Arizona, or New Mexico. They had been active leaders in their congregation in Ohio, Indiana, or Minnesota. When they moved to a warmer climate they dropped out of church.

The reason. When they visited the congregations near their retirement home, they were warmly welcomed. "Oh, you were a leader in your church up north." They were given a list of groupings and volunteer options. *All the options on the list were solid marathon runner options*. They had learned how to be excellent sprinters. So, they dropped out of church and signed up with Habitat for Humanity to do an excellent sprinter project to build one, specific house.

Strong, healthy congregations list, *on the first page* of their groupings and volunteer form, the specific one-time, seasonal, and short-term possibilities. Then, *on the second page,* they list the long-term and weekly, monthly, year-round possibilities. They have more volunteers.

Groupings and Volunteer Possibilities in Our Congregation

Discover with whom you would have fun sharing
            your gifts, strengths, competencies.
What we have fun doing is God's way of teaching us
            our longings, our strengths, our possibilities.

One-Time   Seasonal   Short-Term

*Note: under each heading you would
describe briefly the possibilities.*

Mission

Shepherding

Worship

Fellowship

Common interest

Recreational

Bible study

Prayer gathering

Task force, team

Generous giving

Invite several excellent sprinters to help develop your volunteer list. Yes, some things we have done in marathon ways will now be done in excellent sprinter ways. We will have more volunteers.

NEW

We encourage many new groupings.

Touching Base. More often than not, new people find their way to a congregation in response to the mission outreach or shepherding of the congregation. The congregation is a legend on the community grapevine. Or, the location has open accessibility and high visibility. Something stirs in their heart. They find their way to a service of worship. They "touch base" here. They discover that the service of worship is stirring and helpful. Having shared in the service of worship as few as three or four times, they may begin to look around for a grouping with whom they can share significant relationships of sharing and caring.

Some persons discover their grouping *within the service of worship.* They become part of an informal grouping that has a service of worship as their gathering point. Watch for who visits with whom before and after the service. Look for who has brunch with whom . . . . who carpools their children to school with whom . . . . who begins to share excellent sprinter gatherings together.

A worship service is a collection of informal groupings. It is possible to diagram these informal groupings in a worship service. They provide substantial sharing and caring among the participants. They are among the primary groupings in the life and mission of the congregation. One can diagram them using a collection of circles and, then, provide a brief description of each one. A good deal of the dynamic of the congregation in terms of the sources of stability, change, conflict, and hope can be discovered by a thoughtful understanding of these informal groupings.

New People Join New Groups. New people in a community tend to search out other people who are comparatively new. New people in a congregation tend to search out new groupings in which they can establish relationships of sharing and caring. It is easier for new people to establish close relationships with one another when the network of relationships is still comparatively new, flexible, and in the process of developing.

New groupings have been in existence less than five years. Old groupings have been in existence more than five years. A grouping that has been in existence more than five years has developed a stable, reliable network of relationships. In their half a decade plus of life together, they have created a pattern of relating with one another that is mostly helpful and ingrained.

As genuinely open as the "old grouping" seeks to be, it nevertheless takes new people a while to learn their way and discover their place in an already established network of relationships. Sometimes, their search for community is sufficiently desperate and urgent that they do not have the time to learn the already entrenched network.

It is easier for new people to become part of a new grouping. Its network of relationships is not yet fully in place. Its network is still flexible and fluid. Congregations that encourage new groupings tend to be stable and growing. A congregation that discourages starting new groupings is a church that has decided to die, slowly and eventually . . . .

Not all of the groupings that begin will be successful. Two out of three will likely succeed. Some congregations fail to start new groupings because they have had one or two that failed. As a matter of fact, it is important to do precisely the opposite. The more groupings that have failed, the more important it is to intentionally and thoughtfully encourage an array of new groupings.

Encourage. *We encourage more than start.* Our congregation has the spirit that whoever wants to start a new grouping is welcome to do so. Most quilting groups, community groups, recreational groups, AA groups, and on and on are self-starting groups. Three to five persons discover their common longings and interests. They start a new grouping.

There is no professional staff person. There is no top-down permission granting. There is no deferential "Is it all right?" There is much encouragement. There is much support. The encouragement has the spirit of: "We welcome you to start a new grouping. We do not need to do this for you. We are not interested in developing co-dependent–dependent groupings. This is a congregation that encourages creativity, initiative, self-direction, and self-control."

Yes, leaders in our congregation may gently assist in starting new groupings as well. Having done so, they encourage the new grouping to move forward with its own self-direction and self-initiative. They let the grouping "grow up" and have a life of its own full creation.

Sometimes, in our enthusiasm, we announce that such-and-such a grouping will start at a given time, on a certain day. The announcement is that the group will meet weekly. There is little prior informal conversation or development work. A committee thinks we need a given new group. "You all come."

People do. Regrettably, just enough people who are dysfunctional with one another show up. Now, we invest considerable time, energy, and effort in trying to prop up a group that probably should never have been. The art is to have a one-time gathering. See how it works. See how the group meshes with one another. Have another one-time gathering. Encourage the grouping to develop its own focus and pace of gatherings.

Build. Encourage persons to *build a new grouping on a current, informal relational neighborhood.* We mentioned these at the beginning of the chapter. It is helpful to list them here. The informal, relational neighborhood possibilities include:

> friendship and relational networks
> a life stage
> some human hurt and hope

the same vocational village
a common interest
some community concern
some combination of two or three of the above

Each of these relational neighborhoods provides the "glue" for a new grouping to come together.

The best way to start a new group is to **not** "start" a new group. "Starting" a new group is like inviting people to the marriage before they have had a first date. The way forward is to invite people to a one-time gathering. We encourage them to another one-time gathering. Another. We deepen a sense of relationship. We deepen some common glue. We deepen the sense of home and family, sharing and caring with the lives of the persons God gives us.

DEPTH

People discover a depth of sharing and caring in the groupings of our congregation.

Community, Not Committees. The search for community is the search for roots, place, and belonging—for a grouping of people in which in-depth, significant relationships of sharing and caring take place. We are who we are as a result of the groupings that have informed and enriched our own sense of individuality, of meaning and purpose in life, and of hope for the future. Most people engage in a persistent search for the depth of community that will enrich their lives and enable them to discover and fulfill their life searches.

People search for community, not for committees. People will put up with being on committees to the extent that they have discovered a depth of community. Frequently, the most lively times are *before and after* a committee meeting. People laugh and carry on, stand around and share with one another the sense of community.

In an institutional culture, we would say, "Put John on a committee. He will have ownership for the church." It worked. We put John on a committee. He had ownership for the church. In our time, a movement culture, when we put John on a committee, we are likely on our way to creating a new inactive member. In this time, the first step is to help John discover community in some informal or formal grouping. When John finds home, then he will help.

Community, Not Programs. People are not searching for programs and activities or institutional structures, but for events of compassion, for events of mission, and for experiences of hope in which they can share. They are searching for people with whom they can live out life together. People long for people more than programs.

In an earlier time, we developed a preoccupation with programs and activities. Many communities were new. Not many programs and activities existed in these communities. Local congregations stepped in to fill the vacuum. It worked. People were drawn to congregations because the local church's programs and activities were "the only game in town." The program-centered church was invented. The ballyhoo was, "Something for everyone." It worked!

Time passed.

Communities began to develop extensive programs and activities of their own. Most communities now have more programs and activities than most people could participate in in four lifetimes. People can find a multitude of programs. Amidst all the activities, people long for community.

A Theology of Community. Strong, healthy congregations share a rich, full theology of community. We are a community of covenant . . . . of reconciliation, wholeness, caring, and justice.

We are a sacramental community. When we gather in the grace of God, we are a sacrament. We are a sign of the ever present grace, compassion, community, and hope of God.

We are who we are, because of whose we are. Our depth of sharing and caring is not of our own doing. It is the gift of God. We are a covenantal gathering of informal and formal groupings. Wherever events of grace are experienced, wherever events of compassion happen, wherever events of mission are shared, wherever experiences of hope occur, wherever people live this life's pilgrimage with each other and for the world, there one discovers community.

We search for . . . . long for . . . . community . . . . roots, place, belonging, friends, family, home. Sometimes, we find the community. Sometimes, the community finds us.

We search . . . .
> we search . . . .
> we search for community.

We look around one day and discover the blessing of God's community. We cherish this sacramental gift.

Rating Guide: Significant Relational Groupings

Item	Maximum Points	Our Congregation's Rating
1. Most of our groupings are open, inclusive, warm, and welcoming.	25	_____
2. We have a healthy balance of one-time, seasonal, short-term, long-term, and weekly, monthly, year-round groupings.	25	_____
3. We encourage many new groupings.	25	_____
4. People discover a depth of sharing and caring in the groupings of our congregation.	25	_____
Total	100	_____

Instructions

- Use the resources of this chapter to evaluate your congregation's rating in each of the listed items.
- Enter your rating numbers in the blanks. Then, find the total.
- Divide the total of your score by 10 to obtain your congregation's rating on a scale of 1 to 10.
- Enter your rating of Significant Relational Groupings on the chart in Appendix C on page 258.

Further Resources

Small, Strong Congregations
Twelve Keys for Living
The Twelve Keys Bible Study

5

STRONG LEADERSHIP TEAM

Walter discovered he is a leader.

He said to me, "I have never thought of myself as a leader. I do not have a charismatic personality. I am not a 'charmer.' I am not dynamic and exciting. I am quiet and shy.

"I do not like 'center stage.' What the group tells me is that they do better when I am around."

I shared with Walter my thoughts that many leaders have a gentle humility. They have a passion for the mission. They have the capacity to work with a team. These leaders create lasting groupings that are strong and healthy.

Somewhat quietly, Walter said, "That is me. My grandparents taught me the value of humility. That is who they are. I do have a passion for what we are achieving at work. I guess I get that from my dad and mom. I do have fun with the team we have gathered.

"And, I am still getting use to the idea that this means that I am a leader."

One key, one possibility, for a strong, healthy congregation is a strong leadership team.

A strong, healthy congregation:

- Achieves our key objectives
- Lives the four steps of leadership: loving, listening, learning, and leading
- Encourages the leadership qualities of competency, continuity, and mutual leadership
- Helps people fulfill their life searches

In some efforts, the focus has been on the charismatic, dynamic leader, the pivot point for everything. We are learning, more and more, that lasting movements are led by persons like Walter . . . . and Mary, Gene, Ann, Phil, Teresa, Richard, Elizabeth, Leo, Sylvia, Dan, Pat, Mike, Ken, Shay, Bill, Jonathan . . . . I could go on and on. The list of quiet, compassionate, wise leaders is virtually endless.

ACHIEVE

Our congregation achieves our key objectives.

Achievements, Not Activities. We focus on achievements, not activities. One achievement is worth ten activities. We focus on the current strengths we are expanding and the new strengths we are adding. We achieve our few *key* objectives to expand and add our strengths. We may not achieve all of our objectives. We do achieve our few key objectives. As a result, we continue to grow a strong leadership team.

Too many congregations plan, sponsor, and promote activities that have no direct correlation with their strengths and with the few key objectives and accomplishments toward which they are headed. The more activities a congregation has, the less likely it is to have strong leadership team. It wears its leaders out trying to do too much, too soon.

They waste their precious leader resources in a merry-go-round of activities that whirl faster and faster, and, like a merry-go-round, go nowhere. Activities are never ends in themselves. Key activities are critical events that help us achieve our few key objectives. Achievements come from objectives, not activities.

The Quality of Our Objectives. Some objectives are:

> important and urgent
> important, not urgent
> urgent, not important
> not important, not urgent

A congregation may have a multitude of objectives. Key objectives are important and urgent. Some key objectives are important, not urgent. A range of objectives are urgent, not important. A host of objectives are not important and not urgent.

Our *key* objectives relate to the current strengths we are expanding and the new strengths we are adding. These key objectives are important and urgent. A few of these may be important, and, for now, not urgent.

These key objectives live out the criteria for a solid, key objective:

> match with strengths we are expanding, adding, and sustaining
> written
> strong sense of ownership with grassroots and leaders
> specific and measurable
> realistic time horizons
> an excellent sprinter spirit
> concrete and achievable
> mutually reinforce one another in a complementary fashion

The art of having quality key objectives is the art of focusing on the two out of ten possibilities that will deliver 80 percent of the results.

Generally, a congregation that has too many objectives spreads itself too thin, trying to do too much, too soon, creating a tired, worn-thin, nearly mediocre range of leaders. Too many objectives engender a sense of failure, low self-esteem, and lack of confidence. In healthy congregations, we send in the plays the players can run. We never send in more plays than the players can run. We match the plays to the players.

Recognition and Rewards. We share recognition and rewards. Well done. Well done. Well done. Thank you. Thank you. Thank you. When key objectives are achieved, we are generous with our "Well done" and our "Thank you." We do not say, "You could have done better." We do not say, "You missed this." We thank people when they achieve a key objective.

A positive recognition and reward system creates a strong leader team.

The more a recognition and reward system is preoccupied with negative reinforcement, the more likely that congregation is to have weak, mediocre leaders who suffer from failure, low self-esteem, and lack of confidence. Some recognition and reward systems, in a polite manner, tell people what they are *not* doing.

Such systems grow passive-aggressive behavior, low-grade hostility, subliminal resentment, and eruptive forms of anger. Such systems establish a sense of latent hostility and guilt in a congregation. This sense of hostility and guilt immobilizes people and prevents them from developing their creative, constructive competencies to deliver genuine leadership.

Positive reinforcement any day encourages people more fully than negative reinforcement every day. Under threat, people wither. With encouragement, people grow. They achieve. They accomplish. They move forward. Congregations with a positive recognition and reward system nurture leaders who have compassion and wisdom, common sense and creativity. They are an effective leadership team. These congregations achieve their key objectives.

LIVE

Our congregation lives the four steps of leadership: loving, listening, learning, and leading.

Loving. We love the persons we hope to lead. Now, we are in a stronger position to lead them. It is hard to lead someone we do not love. Compassion casting is the first step toward leading. My saying is, "The team plays well for the coach who loves the team." When we love the team, we can lead the team.

Some teams are easier to love than others. Some have been abused in the past, and, therefore, have learned how to abuse. Some teams have been scared and scarred. Some have experienced dictatorial patterns, and, in turn, have learned how to be dictatorial.

People lead the ways they experience being led.

With some teams, our loving is a gentle, patient loving, much like the loving we share with an abused puppy, fearful and frightened. We do not condone co-dependent and dependent patterns of behavior. Our loving has a spirit of respect. Our loving has boundaries. Our loving is not a "willy-nilly, gushy, maudlin, syrupy sentimentality." Our loving is rich and full, respectful and generous.

Listening. When we love someone, we listen. We are interested in them. We are interested in their excellent ideas and good suggestions, their hopes and their aspirations. We listen well. We do not talk. We listen. We do not interrupt with "I hear you saying . . . ." We listen.

We listen at three levels. One, we listen for what people are saying. We pay close attention. Two, we listen between the lines. We listen for hidden meanings. Three, we listen for what people do not say. I visit with a couple. They talk on and on about their first-born son, and all of the wondrous things he is doing. They say nothing about their other two children. I have learned much about the dynamics of the family by what is not said.

One of the sacramental gifts you can share with people is the gift of listening. In our busy, bustling, frantic times, hardly anyone listens. We rush here and there. We are busy with this and that. We give people a sacred, precious gift when we stop . . . . when we listen.

Learning. When we listen, we learn. We do not learn when we are talking. We can only learn when we are listening. Sometimes, we allow our gift for teaching, our gift for telling, and our gift for advising to overtake our gift for learning. In our eagerness to help, we try to help before we have listened well . . . . before we have learned well.

Learning is the art of creative listening. We ask ourselves, "What is this person trying to teach me?" Sometimes, what they are saying and what they are trying to teach have a close correlation with one another. Sometimes, what they are saying and what they are really trying to teach us are far apart. We ask ourselves, "What are we really learning here?"

Leaders are learners. Leaders value the gift of learning. They appreciate how extraordinary the gift of learning is. They cherish the people from whom they learn. They long for new possibilities for learning. They look to the present and the future for what they can learn.

Leading. We love. We listen. We learn. We lead. Some persons skip the first three steps. They seek to lead before they have loved, listened, and learned. They are eager to help. They believe their leadership will help. They want to do good work. They think they have a way forward. They set out to lead.

They have not earned the integrity, trust, and mutual respect of the persons they seek to lead. They have not shared the richness of their love. They have not taken time to listen. They have not learned the dynamics of the congregation. Their leading feels like pushing and shoving, not leading. Resistance develops. The leader increases and presses his leadership efforts.

Matters escalate. Now, we spend time unraveling what was a truncated effort to lead.

It takes less time to love, listen, and learn. It takes more time, energy, and effort to untruncate, to redevelop a situation that has gone awry. Some people have said words they wish they had not said. They wish they could take them back. Excess breeds excess. It is easier to love, listen, learn, and lead. These four steps contribute to a grouping being a strong leader team.

ENCOURAGE

We encourage the leadership qualities of competency, continuity, and mutual leadership.

Competency.   Leaders are competent *as leaders. Leaders lead.* We are competent leaders, not enablers, not managers. In the churched culture of an earlier time, it was possible for the church to focus on developing enablers or being managers. It was "the thing to do" to go to church. People sought out the church. It was easier to be an enabler. It was easier to be a manager. Enablers do good work. Managers do good work. Our current mission culture encourages persons to be competent leaders.

The leadership philosophy centered on the "enabler" was a major contribution. It worked over against a dictatorial, benevolent authoritarian style of leadership. It was a useful counterpoint. However, when the enabler concept was linked to nondirective counseling techniques, teams suffered from less than competent leadership. A responsive, process-centered style of leadership contributed to congregations being weak, declining, or dying.

The leadership philosophy that created "managers" was a major contribution. There was need for managers to develop policies and procedures, rules and regulations, conditions and stipulations. Managers keep "chaos" at bay. Managers do excellent work at regulating and managing "what is." In our time, we need leaders who will help us discover "what will be" . . . . to help us grow forward . . . . to discover the mission to which God is inviting us.

Leaders lead a congregation to achieve and accomplish key objectives. They benefit enablers and managers. Leaders are active as well as responsive. They are proactive as well as reactive. Leaders share their own sense of direction, as well as helping others to share theirs. Leaders are thoughtful and responsible, and they share with the grassroots, with compassion, wisdom, and integrity.

Competent leaders are not dictatorial and authoritarian, even in the most benevolent ways. They do not manipulate the decision process in covert ways. Congregations benefit from more leaders, fewer enablers, fewer managers, and fewer still dictators.

In strong, healthy congregations, there is an excellent match between the competent leaders, their key objectives, and their authority. These qualities contribute to this excellent match. The leader has:

> compassion for persons, this congregation, and its mission in the world
>
> passion for the key objective, with a spirit of hope
>
> wisdom and discernment, common sense and good judgment
>
> general competencies for constructive work patterns
>
> excellent sprinter and solid marathon capacities
>
> specific competencies that match well with the key objective to be achieved
>
> a constructive spirit in both productive and stress and conflict situations
>
> a spirit of grace, character, integrity, trust, thoughtfulness, and mutual respect

When a person has five of these eight qualities well in place, the person is a good match with a specific key objective.

As they move forward to achieve their key objective, some of the remaining three will grow forward as well.

A healthy congregation, first, discovers the number of leaders it has. It uses the eight qualities above to discover potential leaders. Then, we build our key objectives in direct relation to the number and strengths of our leaders. Having "vacant slots" is a symptom that a congregation is first developing its plays, then trying to match its players to its plays. Unfortunately, some churches decide their activities as though they had an unlimited reservoir of leaders.

A congregation sets itself up for success when it takes seriously how many leaders are present and the range of their competencies, then builds its key objectives. A few churches are innocently masochistic. They decide their programs and organization, then try to squeeze their leaders into preordained programs and organization. They "enjoy" the sense of failure and low self-esteem such a process engenders. They commit themselves to a "filling of the empty slots" and to a limping, disastrous disarray of disappointment and failure.

We *first* discover the number of competent players who show up for practice, and what they do best. *Then,* we design the plays to match. No wise football coach or choir director does it the other way around. The coach thinks of what the players do best. The coach also thinks of the new plays that the players can learn. The coach "bridges" the players to any new plays based on what they do best. Excellent choir directors do the same. We have this spirit. We are competent as leaders. We are competent to achieve key objectives.

Creative Continuity. There is a correlation between competency and continuity. With a key objective, it sometimes takes continuity—time—to achieve the objective. Strong, healthy congregations give leaders time to achieve their key objective. *We encourage creative continuity.*

Frequently, it takes some time to achieve a given key objective. In stage one, the person is learning "the ground." In stage two, the person is gathering their leader team. In stage three, they are "beginning" to hit their stride. They come into their own in stage four and stage five.

Competency and continuity are good friends. Some churches focus on who is willing, on who is committed. There is a diversity of gifts. Some people are "willing" to be pitcher. Their competencies are at shortstop. We do not build a winning team by giving everyone the chance to pitch. We do give everyone the chance to play in the game—at a position matching their strengths. We develop a winning combination of competency and continuity.

Persons who are authoritarian are not leaders. They are dictators. We do not focus on them. We have an appropriate fear of persons who tend toward a dictatorial, authoritarian style. They do damage and harm. They deny the leadership strengths of other leaders and of the grassroots.

We focus on persons who are competent leaders. They have strong objective-setting and process-development skills. They have compassion and wisdom. We share with them the gift of authority and the gift of continuity. They are having fun. They are enjoying what they are achieving. We are enjoying what they are achieving.

We leave them alone. We stay out of their way. We do not slow them down. We do not demotivate them. We say "Well done." We thank them.

We encourage people to "move on" when:

> they have achieved their key objective
> they are no longer having fun
> they are no longer "growing in the work"
> they are no longer achieving a specific key objective
> we think they have achieved about what they can accomplish

We help them discover a new objective they can achieve and have fun doing. Some people stay too long in a post. More people are asked to move on just about the time they are coming into their own. Continuity means we are not drawn to the temptation, "It is working. It is not broken. We had better fix it." We do not fix what is not broken. We do not fix what is working.

Mutual Leadership. *We are mutual with the persons we serve.* We build a strong leadership team for the total persons we serve. With a mutual spirit, we serve members, constituents, persons served in mission, friends of our congregation who live elsewhere, and community persons. We serve them as a whole family God gives us to serve.

We do not build a leadership team to serve members only. Many leader teams feel overworked, battle-fatigued, blurry eyed, and burned out because they are. The team was built to serve members. In fact, the team is serving five groupings, not one. A strong, healthy congregation deals with far more people in a year's time than simply its members. We build a leadership team to serve "the whole family."

We share a balance of mutual strengths. A healthy leadership team draws on, honors, and benefits from including persons with these complementary strengths:

compassion—shepherding, sharing, caring, generosity
community—good fun, good times, social, relational, covenantal, family
hope—encouraging, possibilities, confidence, assurance
wisdom—discerning, thoughtful, analytical, commonsense
leading—stirring, grassroots, common action

These strengths contribute to a strong, healthy leader team. We include, respect, and benefit from these mutual strengths. We have balance with each strength present on the leader team.

We are a mutual team. As grassroots, leaders, pastor, and staff, we are a mutual leader team. We build a team to serve the total persons served. We honor one another's gifts. We work together as a whole team. We achieve our key objectives, mutually, as a whole family. We do not have hierarchical layers, detailed organizational charts, and minute, distinct, compartmental structures. We do not live in silos. We do not say, "This is my department."

The objective shapes the organization. The strategy shapes the structure. We share mutual key objectives. The key objective shapes how we work together. The organization does not shape how we work together. We begin with the key objective, not some latent organizational structure.

There is a diversity of gifts. We have our distinct gifts, but there are no higher or lower levels. The staff and the pastor serve, mutually, with the grassroots and leaders of the congregation. We are not a staff-centered congregation nor a lay-centered congregation. We are in this venture together. We are mutual. We are one mutual family—grassroots, leaders, pastor, and staff.

FULFILL

We help people fulfill their life searches.

God blesses us with wondrous gifts. God gives us the gift of life. We are alive, not by accident, but as a gift of God. We could not have been born. We breathe . . . . and move . . . . and live . . . . and have our being as God's gift. We cherish the gift of life. We are amazed with God's generosity. We are alive through the grace of God.

God gives us the gift of life searches. God plants within our hearts these yearnings . . . . these longings . . . . these searches. These life searches draw us closer to God. God does not give us the gift of life, and, then, leave us alone . . . . to figure our own way forward . . . . by ourselves. These life searches are God's way of helping us to find God . . . . to live whole, healthy lives in the grace of God. These life searches lead us to God.

Leaders are leaders because they help persons fulfill their life searches.

Leaders *help*. Leaders, finally, cannot fulfill these life searches for someone. It is their pilgrimage. It is their opportunity to fulfill their own life searches. We share experience and wisdom. We share possibilities. We share compassion. We encourage. We bless. We share almost enough help to be helpful, but not so much help that the help becomes harmful and creates a co-dependent–dependent pattern of behavior. We share confidence and assurance that persons have the resources . . . . the abilities to fulfill their life searches.

One or two of these life searches are primary at a given point in one's life pilgrimage. All are present in each person. You can grow and develop, advance and build any of these life searches. Usually, one or two tend to be pressing . . . . to be predominant. Now. Later, it may be another one or two. Life is a pilgrimage. Life is a search. For now, it is these one or two searches.

Leaders, and strong, healthy congregations, help persons fulfill the one or two life searches pressing for this time.

Grace. We long for grace. We search for grace. We realize we have fallen short of the glory of God. We sense the sin within us. We have engaged in our full share of sin. We anguish. We regret. We feel torment. We suffer ourselves with the memories of sinful events.

We seek mercy and forgiveness. We long for grace.

Compassion. We yearn for compassion. We long for sharing, caring, giving, loving, serving. We want to give compassion as well as receive compassion. We discover that in giving compassion, we receive compassion several fold. The giving results in the receiving. The receiving results in the giving.

Community. We search for roots, place, and belonging. We want to share in good fun and good times. We long for wedding feasts of community and great banquets of family. We sense our loneliness . . . . our fragmentation . . . . our separateness. We feel our despair. We have a desperate search for community. We long for home.

Individuality. We yearn for individuality—for a sense of identity, autonomy, integrity, and power in our existence and destiny. We do not want to feel powerless . . . . to feel that all the decisions that shape our lives are made by someone else somewhere else and we cannot quite find out who or why. We want some sense that *some* of the decisions that affect our lives and shape our destinies are made by us . . . . that we have some say as individuals over our own lives.

Meaning. We search for meaning—for the discovery of values in everyday life. Meaning has something to do with reasonability . . . . with data, analysis, logic, and purpose. Meaning has to do with passion. Meaning has to do with creativity. With a longing passion, we discover our understanding of everyday, ordinary life in the light of the grace of God.

Hope. We long for hope. We search for a reliable and certain present and future. We long for confidence and assurance in the grace of God. We look for hope in the present. If we cannot find hope in the present, we postpone our hopes down the road. We look for hope in the immediate future . . . . in the distant future . . . . with God in the next life future beyond the River.

We live on hope, not memory. Memory is strong. Hope is stronger. Take away a person's memories and they become anxious. Take away a person's hopes and they become terrified.

Memory is strong because memory is about everyday, ordinary life events, celebrative events, tragic events, sinful events, and hope-fulfilling events. Memory is strong primarily because memory remembers hope-fulfilling events . . . . the Passover . . . . the Exodus . . . . the Incarnation . . . . the Crucifixion . . . . the Open Tomb, the Risen Lord, and New Life in Christ. We live on hope. Our hope is in the grace of God . . . . for the present . . . . for the immediate and distant future . . . . and for the next life future beyond the River. Hope is stronger than memory. Leaders lead with hope.

Persons become leaders as they achieve key objectives . . . . as they live the four steps of leadership . . . . as they encourage leadership qualities . . . . as they help people fulfill their life searches. They coach. They share wisdom and experience. They encourage. They stir and inspire. They bless. They are a strong leadership team.

Rating Guide: Strong Leadership Team

Item	Maximum Points	Our Congregation's Rating
1. Our congregation achieves our key objectives.	25	_____
2. Our congregation lives the four steps of leadership: loving, listening, learning, and leading.	25	_____
3. We encourage the leadership qualities of competency, continuity, and mutual leadership.	25	_____
4. We help people fulfill their life searches.	25	_____
Total	100	_____

Instructions

- Use the resources of this chapter to evaluate your congregation's rating in each of the listed items.
- Enter your rating numbers in the blanks. Then, find the total.
- Divide the total of your score by 10 to obtain your congregation's rating on a scale of 1 to 10.
- Enter your rating of Strong Leadership Team on the chart in Appendix C on page 258.

Further Resources

Effective Church Leadership
The Future That Has Come
Small, Strong Congregations
The Twelve Keys Bible Study

6

SOLID DECISION PROCESS

"We made the right decision. We made it the wrong way. Everyone agrees it was the right decision. Hardly anyone has ownership for the decision. We learned from this that two things are important: the wisdom of the decision and the process whereby the decision is made."

Harold was sharing his experience with me.

He went on to say, "Sometimes, we make the wrong decision. And, we make it the wrong way. Now, we are doubly foiled. And, yes, we have been known to make the wrong decision in the right way. At least, we have wide ownership for the wrong decision.

"With our present dilemma, it seems hard to know what to do. We have been in this kind of fix before. I hope it works out."

One key, one possibility, for a strong, healthy congregation is a solid decision process.

A strong, healthy congregation:

- Makes wise, thoughtful decisions in relation to our key objectives
- Has a strong sense of openness and ownership in our decision process

- Shares a spirit of integrity, mutual respect, and trust with one another
- Has a simple structure based on our key objectives

In some groupings, the focus is primarily on making the right decision. In some, the focus is on the process. Any solid decision process honors both. In doing so, you encourage the decision process to be a gift of grace in the lives of the people who are part of the process.

DECISIONS

The purpose of process is decisions. We share almost enough discussion that we achieve wise decisions. The purpose of discussion is not discussion. Frequently, the more discussion we have, the more confused we become. We value a certain range of data and demographics. Sometimes, the more data and demographics we gather, and the more discussions we have, the more confused we become. We develop analysis paralysis. We develop discussion paralysis.

The art is to share and discuss. Discuss and share. Perhaps, a third time. We decide. We move forward. We act . . . . swiftly.

Our decisions reflect wisdom and judgment, compassion and common sense. Sometimes, a congregation develops decisions that are simply faddish, reflecting a popular fad among churches that is momentarily, fleetingly, sweeping across the country. Sometimes, a congregation develops decisions that are immature, hastily reached on the spur of the moment. They reflect an adolescent rather than an adult sense of wisdom and discernment.

Sometimes, churches successfully achieve decisions that are excellent mistakes. The decisions reflect neither wisdom nor common sense. Often, such decisions are made because the church has allowed someone to sell them "a bill of goods," or the congregation has not thought through the "unintended consequences" of the decision. Generally, decisions are solid decisions when they reflect deep compassion, sound wisdom, helpful judgment, and thoughtful common sense.

Our decisions focus on important priorities rather than urgent trivialities. It is helpful to think of four groups of decisions that congregations consider:

A level decisions	important and urgent
B level decisions	important, not urgent
C level decisions	urgent, not important
D level decisions	neither important nor urgent

Healthy congregations invest most of their decision time on A level and B level decisions. Some churches live out their lives preoccupied with C and D level decisions. Then, they wonder why they are weak, declining, or dying congregations.

Our "A level decisions" focus on:

the strengths we claim
the one or two current strengths we plan to expand
the one or two new strengths we plan to add
the current strengths we plan to sustain
the key objectives with which we will act swiftly

Our decisions have character. We focus on decisions that are needed as well as those that are wanted. Our decisions reflect courage and backbone. They are not willy-nilly efforts to please everyone—which usually end up pleasing no one. We share maturity in our decisions.

PROCESS

Openness and ownership are good friends. Openness breeds ownership. Ownership encourages openness. The more openness in our decision process, the more ownership people have for the decisions. The more ownership for the decisions, the more open people are with their compassion and wisdom, their excellent ideas and good suggestions. Healthy congregations have a strong sense of openness and ownership in their process of making decisions.

Every congregation has both informal and formal networks of conversation about decisions. There are informal, grassroots conversations. There are formal, structural conversations. In healthy congregations, these major networks of conversation have a genuine openness with one another. The informal, grassroots process of making decisions and the formal, structural process of making decisions "talk" with one another. The key decisions are open decisions . . . . with both the informal and formal networks sharing in constructive conversation with one another.

The process is open and inclusive rather than closed and restricted. That does not mean that every person should be forced to participate in every decision. There existed, some years ago, a fad for total consensus on every decision. You can give up the notion that everyone should be included in every decision—or that everyone *wants* to be included in every decision. Most people do not. Rather, they want a sense of openness and inclusiveness that makes it easy for them to share their own wisdom on a given matter if they want to do so.

Everyone is encouraged to participate in the central, strategic decisions that shape the present and future of the congregation. Whether we have yellow or blue name tags at our next Wednesday night covered dish supper, someone is free to decide. What we are interested in are the major decisions on the strengths we claim, the current strength we plan to expand, and the new strength we plan to add.

We are interested in where we are heading in our present and our future. People do not like any hint that the decision process is secretive and restrictive. People do not participate in congregations where a few people, almost in closed, restrictive ways, make the key decisions. Then, this small group "farms out" the minor decisions to the very people they have excluded from the key decisions. People do not participate in such a congregation.

Most key decisions are arrived at in informal conversations, then ratified in the formal structure. This is not subterfuge or a covert pattern of behavior. Many people make most of the decisions they make in everyday life in informal settings and informal discussions. The marriage proposal takes place in an informal setting. The wedding takes place in a formal setting. In making decisions in the life of a congregation, people follow the same behavior patterns.

We give people sufficient lead time to discuss informally with one another a major decision before they are called upon to make the decision in a formal gathering. The key leaders and pastor encourage a rich connection between the informal, grapevine conversations and the more formal structures of the church. Decisions are discussed on the grapevines, then brought to the formal structures for ratification.

The decision leads to the action.

We encourage both the process and the resulting decisions. The process by which we achieve a decision is as important as the decision itself. Our decision process drives toward decisions, not discussion, toward accomplishments and achievements, not a blur of activities. We move forward, confident that the process and decisions will facilitate future decisions and directions.

INTEGRITY

Integrity breeds mutual respect. Mutual respect breeds trust. Both our decisions and our process encourage integrity, mutual respect, and trust. Our integrity, mutual respect, and trust encourage us to develop solid decisions and an open process.

When the qualities of integrity, mutual respect, and trust are shared in a congregation, we will deal constructively with any conflict that may arise. People are bound to have some differences of opinion. Some may think that a given direction is helpful for our congregation. By the same token, some may think another direction is more helpful.

Amidst differing ways forward, the art is to grow integrity, mutual respect, and trust. Yes, we invest some energy in conflict resolution. We invest more time in growing the qualities of integrity, mutual respect, and trust. What will see us through the conflict is our sense of integrity with one another. If you have a choice, and you do, focus more on growing integrity and less on dealing with conflict. Indeed, the primary way to deal with conflict is to grow integrity.

Stability, change, conflict, and hope are persistent, useful, creative dynamics in the life of the congregation. Healthy congregations develop the capacity to resolve rather than repress conflict. A congregation has an effective decision process when the members—in the midst of conflict over a given matter—respond to one another with integrity, mutual respect, and trust. A discussion of the principles and purposes rather than an attack on personalities demonstrates a congregation with an effective spirit of integrity, mutual respect, and trust with one another.

This is not to say that people will not shout at each other. Sometimes, they will. This is not to say that people will not sometimes spread gossip about their opponents in the conflict. They frequently do so. Rumors abound. And, over the long haul, a congregation that has a helpful decision-making process is one in which members, even amidst a raging conflict, share with each other an inviting sense of integrity, mutual respect and trust . . . . with a spirit of grace.

Our process . . . . with grace takes seriously the anxiety level present within people. Most of the time, our anxiety level has a natural ebb and flow. Surprise us with a new proposal, out of the blue, with no advance warning, or gentle coaching. Our anxiety level soars . . . . skyrockets. We become preoccupied with getting our anxiety level back down to normal. The new proposal caused the anxiety level to skyrocket. Thus, we reject the new proposal, not because we are inherently against it, but in order to get our anxiety level back down to normal.

In a healthy process, major proposals are not surprises. They are shared gently and thoughtfully. We give people sufficient time to mull them over. Frequently, very good proposals are rejected because they have been hurriedly, hastily shared with people, who are asked for an immediate decision. Major proposals need several days, weeks, or months of "mulling over" before people can bring their anxiety level down to normal and deal with the proposal itself.

Then, after adequate time for informal conversations has passed, we bring the matter to a more formal gathering for discussion and decision. People know in advance the decisions they will be called upon to make. They will deal with their anxiety levels. They will, creatively and constructively, think through the best alternatives and possibilities related to a given decision.

We honor people with integrity, mutual respect, and trust. To honor people is to give them both key objectives and authority. We do not honor them when we give them objectives and little or no authority. Authority is a matter of integrity, mutual trust, and respect. We encourage the qualities of integrity, mutual respect, and trust with one another and in our congregation.

SIMPLE

We have a simple structure. Our streamlined organizational structure is based on our congregation's major key objectives. Objectives shape organization. Function determines form. Decisions determine design. Strategy shapes structure. Where we are headed shapes how we organize to get there.

We claim our strengths. We decide on one or two current strengths to expand and one or two new strengths to add. We sustain our current strengths. We create a simple structure to achieve our key objectives.

Structure expands to fill the time available. The more time we allow ourselves, the more complex the structure becomes. We invest just enough time to move forward, but not so much time that the structure becomes the objective. We can always modify, change, and improve our structure as we move forward.

We have just enough of a structure that we accomplish our objectives. Our structure feels like a fast break down a basketball court, not a neat, tidy, slowly unfolding plan that barely moves. We have just enough teams to develop strong achievements. Each grouping has enough members to move forward. We achieve creative decisions and effective action.

The purpose of a congregation is to involve people in:

living a whole, healthy life in the grace of God
God's mission in the world
shepherding that is compassionate and restoring
stirring, helpful worship
a grouping where they find home

The purpose is not to involve people in meeting after meeting. A person can be significantly involved in any one or two of these above and spend very little time coming to meetings. Some congregations consume so much of an individual's time in meetings that they have very little time left over to participate in that church's mission in the world. Healthy congregations conserve their members' time. They develop a minimal, streamlined organizational structure. This way people can be involved, richly and fully, in the total life and mission of the congregation.

We move forward with confidence and competence. We share genuine momentum, solid competencies, and excellent results. We benefit from the power of wise, compassionate decisions. We are grateful to God for leading us to the future that God is both promising and preparing for us.

Rating Guide: Solid Decision Process

Item	Maximum Points	Our Congregation's Rating
1. We make wise, thoughtful decisions in relation to our key objectives.	25	_____
2. We have a strong sense of openness and ownership in our decision process.	25	_____
3. We share a spirit of integrity, mutual respect, and trust with one another.	25	_____
4. We have a simple structure based on our key objectives.	25	_____
	_____	_____
Total	100	_____

Instructions

- Use the resources of this chapter to evaluate your congregation's rating in each of the listed items.
- Enter your rating numbers in the blanks. Then, find the total.
- Divide the total of your score by 10 to obtain your congregation's rating on a scale of 1 to 10.
- Enter your rating of Solid Decision Process on the chart in Appendix C on page 258.

Further Resources

Effective Church Leadership
The Future That Has Come
Small, Strong Congregations
The Twelve Keys Bible Study

7

ONE MAJOR PROGRAM

With thoughtful, quiet determination, Sue said, "We like being busy . . . . We just don't like being this bussssssssy. Choir practice. Soccer. Homework. Band practice. Club meetings. Homework. Scouts. Youth Group. Homework. Car pools here. Car pools there. Meetings to plan meetings. The list goes on and on. It feels like a merry-go-round. And the next school year looks even bussierrrrrrrr.

"Busyness expands to fill the time available. And, we ran out of time." Sue sighed.

"Time has become our most precious asset. We value our time more than ever before. We have come to realize that 'things' matter less. People matter more. And, it is the time we have with people that matters the most. It has taken us too many years to discover this fact.

"We spend and waste time as though we had a million years.

"We decided to do something about it. We have. We now find time for one another. We sense how precious the time we have is for us. We are grateful for the quiet grace of God in our lives. We no longer rush here and there.

"It is not that we gave up being busy. It is not that we quit doing so many activities. It is that we decided to live more fully with one another, to cherish one another more dearly, to savor . . . . to enjoy . . . . to embrace the time we have with one another.

"It is not what we gave up. It is what we have found . . . . each other.

"The grace of God is blessing our lives together."

The room was silent. A hush. A stillness. Then, a rush of applause as people stood, laughing and clapping. Sue had gathered the feelings and hopes of the whole group.

One key, one possibility, for a strong, healthy congregation is one major program.

A strong, healthy congregation:

- Has one major program that is among the best in the community
- Serves many persons and families in the church with this one program
- Has leaders who are both person centered and program centered
- Has one major program that has some connection with our one major mission outreach

Now, before we discuss the key of one major program, it will help to share a word on the distinctions between mission and program. Later in this chapter, I will share something of the connection between the two.

The primary distinction is *the beginning focus* of each. A mission outreach begins primarily to serve persons *in the community*. This originating focus shapes the direction of the venture. We begin with the community. We serve well. On the other hand, a program venture begins primarily to serve persons *in the congregation*. We begin with the congregation. We serve well.

Where we begin shapes how we serve.

Distinctions

One Helpful, Legendary, Mission Outreach	One Major Program
The beginning focus is to serve persons and groupings in the community.	The beginning focus is to serve persons and groupings in the congregation.
The mission serves directly persons and groupings in the community.	The program serves directly persons and groupings in the church.
Many leaders and volunteers come from both the community and the congregation.	Many leaders and volunteers come from the congregation.
The place or places of the mission happen in the community as well as the church.	The place or places of the program happen in the church.
The resources and funding come from the generosity of both the community and the congregation.	The resources and funding come from the generosity of the congregation.

Some call a given program a mission. In reality, it serves primarily persons in the congregation. Calling something a mission does not make it a mission. Likewise, some ventures in mission are called programs, when, in fact, they serve persons and groupings in the community, and no one from the congregation participates. Some ventures serve both the community and the congregation. As we move through our discussion, the suggestions in the chapter will help.

ONE

A congregation has this central characteristic well in place when it has one major program that is among the best in the community.

In an earlier time, there were few programs available in the community. The church was a primary source of programs and activities . . . . for all of life. Many communities have many programs now. In our time, congregations have this characteristic well in place when they have one major, competent program that has a community-wide respect and competency.

People serve people. There is a myth among some congregations that the more programs and activities a church can offer, the more people it will serve in the community. The likelihood of that happening is remote. Program is the seventh central characteristic, not the first. Any two of the first four—mission, shepherding, worship, or groupings—will be more valuable in helping a congregation to be strong and healthy.

People can find "home" in a grouping within a congregation. The grouping does not also have to be a program with community-wide respect and integrity. Many people find home in the adult choir, without that choir also being among the best adult choirs in the whole community. Many youth find "home" in the congregation's youth grouping without that youth group also being among the best youth programs in the community.

When you do *not* have a multiplicity of programs and activities, this is God's way of blessing you. Now, most communities have more programs and activities than most people could participate in in four lifetimes. The more programs and activities a church offers, the more fatigued and overworked the leaders and pastor of a congregation become.

A mission-giving congregation is more helpful than a program-driven congregation.

I help congregations in Florida, Arizona, and New Mexico who say to me, "Dr. Callahan, we have no one in our congregation under sixty-five years of age." They are working out of the notion that the only way a congregation can be effective and successful is to have people of all ages—cradle to the grave.

I respond by saying, "The reason there are no people in your congregation under sixty-five years of age is because there are no people in the community under sixty-five years of age. In some congregations in Florida, the children's division is for persons sixty-five to seventy-five. The youth program is for persons seventy-five to eighty-five. The adult program is for persons eighty-five and above."

The new children and youth who will see to the future of this congregation are the new "children and youth" who will retire from Ohio, Indiana, Illinois, and Pennsylvania to those sections of Florida over the years to come. These congregations are best off in developing the best early retirement program in their communities, not a children or youth program.

Congregations who have this strength in place share one program that provides major resources with members and constituents of the congregation. The focus may be a:

human hurt and hope
life stage
common interest
community concern
some combination

It might be the preschool program, the early retired program, the music program, the scout program, the basketball program, the quilting program, and so on.

The congregation's major program is measured by the community-wide standards of competence for this kind of program. Regrettably, some congregations have a "soft" analytical, evaluative perspective as they assess their major program. They evaluate their program through rose-colored glasses, based on their own uncritical self-satisfaction with what they have developed.

Many congregations decide the major program will be the music program. They measure the stature of their music program by the critical standards and criteria prevalent in the various music fields in the community. We look at our music program in comparison to:

other church music programs
educational music programs

civic music programs

commercial music programs

general standards for excellence in the field of music prevailing in the community

People do not assess their congregation's music program only in relation to other church music programs. Indeed, it is often the case that church people are not very familiar with what is taking place in other church music programs. But it is clearly the case that most people—both churched and community—experience music in the educational, civic, and commercial arenas of the community. They assess the church music program in relation to the experiences of music they have in day-to-day living.

When a congregation intentionally decides to develop one major program, it helps for the congregation to plan on four to five years of development. It takes a considerable investment of leadership, time, and money to put in place the quality and caliber of a major program.

It takes four to five years to build a major program. It takes this long to develop a professional football team into a winning, pro team. If it takes that long to develop winning competencies in something, finally, as simple as professional football, it is not surprising that it takes at least four to five years to develop a major program to help people with their complex hurts and hopes, plans and directions, disappointments and accomplishments in this life's pilgrimage on earth.

MANY

Our one major program serves many persons and families.

Our one major program has competent quality and considerable quantity. We deliver both quality and quantity. A "minor" program might have exquisite quality and serve a modest number of persons. An "elective" might have modest quality and serve a few persons. Our one major program serves a considerable number of constituents and members. A constituent is a "formal nonmember" who participates in some activity of the congregation. It can be shepherding, worship, a grouping, or a program. Many constituents, because of their participation, think of themselves as "informal members."

"Many" is a relative term. In a small village, "many" would be a certain range of people. In a county seat town, "many" would be another range of people. In a large city, "many" would be yet another range of people. The rubric is: the size of the group is large enough to "hold its own" with the size of the community. In a small village, a preschool program that involves thirty children is likely "holding its own." In a large city, a preschool program serving 120 to 200 children is more likely "holding its own."

These numbers are illustrative. Do not get caught up in them. The point is that for a program to be thought of as a major program, it needs to include a sufficient number of persons to "hold its own" in the community in which it lives . . . . to have consequence in the community.

A congregation's one major program is multidimensional. For example, a major music program serves a range of groups and age levels and a diversity of musical possibilities. It does not focus on a narrow age range or a select group. It may have started out that way in earlier years. Now, the program is attractive because of its competence, and it draws multiple groups and age levels.

When a congregation develops one major program, it benefits from two spillover impacts. First, with one major program well in place, the other programs in the congregation tend to rise toward its level of competence. The greater the competence of that one major program, the more likely that some of the other programs will rise to that level of competence.

The second spillover impact is that people in the community *assume* that the church's other programs offer a comparable degree of excellence. In many churches the preschool program is highly regarded on the grapevine as the finest in the community.

Some of these families visit the worship service, assuming the worship service will be likely of the same quality as the pre-school program. The community's impression of a church's total program is formed by their perception of the one major program for which the congregation is well known in the community.

PERSON CENTERED . . . . PROGRAM CENTERED

The leaders of our one major program are both person centered and program centered.

A program becomes a major program because of this combination. The leaders bring sound relational competencies. In a major music program, the key leaders have relational competencies that enable them to direct with compassion and excellent human relations skills. They have functional competencies in music as well. They bring sound musical training. The combination of relational and functional competencies is well in place; thus, there is a strong tendency for the program to emerge as the one major program in the life of a congregation.

It is wise to select leaders who have **both** relational and functional skills for a program the congregation decides to make its one major program. Regrettably, a vast number of churches select program leaders just on the basis of the functional competencies they bring to the program. Or, they select leaders who have relational skills, but not functional skills. These persons coddle the kids, but this does not create excellence in a program. We select leaders who have both strong, healthy relational and functional competencies.

The key is persons. We focus on the persons participating in our one major program. We focus on the excellence of the program. We do both . . . . with a dynamic balance. We are both person centered and program centered.

CONNECTION

Our one major program has some connection with our one, major, specific, concrete mission.

With the distinctions I mentioned at the beginning of the chapter, I do want to confirm that one can develop a "common ground" connection between a mission and a program. Our mission is with children in a low-income housing project. We have the best Vacation Bible School program in our congregation. The "common ground" is that both have to do with children.

We have a life stage connection, *a bridge*. We could have a bridge centered on a specific human hurt and hope, or a common interest, or a community concern. A disconnected venture would be to have a mission that focuses on slum gangs and a major program that focuses on early retired persons. There might be a remote connection between these two, but it is distant.

Consider an emphasis with youth. The commonality is that both the mission and the program focus on youth. This life stage is the connection. The point of differentiation is that community youth and church youth can be very dissimilar. They can have very distinct:

goals and values
customs, habits, and traditions
styles of dress and behavior
language and communication networks
leadership and decision-making processes
sacred places of meeting
common shared vision of the future

The art is to have a mission and a program that bridge to each other . . . . with a sufficient connection that each helps the other. Congregations develop an informal, indirect connection, or a formal, direct connection between their one specific, concrete mission and the one major program they have in place. Most often, this connection is a relational, friendship connection between some of the leaders and grassroots in both the community and the congregation.

When this happens, we create a spirit of serving both persons in the community and persons in the congregation. There is interchange. People are part of one, then move to participate in the other. There is "mutual belonging." People participate in both a mission and a program.

A congregation is wise to think through the possibility that one major mission and one major program complement and supplement one another. This mutual reinforcement strengthens both. Not every mission need have a matching program that the church has developed. Not every program in a congregation needs to have a connection with a mission. At the same time, such mutual reinforcement, when it is natural and beneficial, is helpful.

Some congregations have too many programs. The pastors and leaders are so busily involved in spinning their merry-go-round of programs . . . . faster and faster . . . . the blur of activities moves swifter and swifter . . . . that they have hardly any time left to participate in one major mission outreach in the world.

They behave like a Bo-Peep church. They take the stance of passively waiting for unchurched people to participate in the smorgasbord of programs that they offer *inside* the church. The message is, "We are here. We are waiting on you to find us. Come to us."

Little Bo-Peep has lost her sheep,
But leave them alone,
And they will come home,
Wagging their tails behind them.

Bo-Peep congregations do not seek out persons in the community. They leave them alone. The many committee meetings, planning sessions, busy programs, and bustling activities prevent people from being genuinely, authentically involved in mission in the community.

To some extent, this excessive investment of leaders, time, and money in programs is fostered by the desire for safety and security. It is safer and more secure to invest one's leadership, time, and money in the quiet safety of activities *inside* a local church than it is to seek out lost people in rough, rocky places of life and share with them help and hope. Because of the factors of safety and security, we may always have some Bo-Peep congregations with us.

God encourages us to live as Good Shepherd congregations, willing to seek out the lost and lonely . . . . the troubled and disturbed . . . . the sick and infirmed . . . . as General Booth of the Salvation Army would say . . . . the "whomsoever of the earth." Congregations serve God's kingdom better as they focus on developing one major program rather than a merry-go-round of activities spinning faster and faster until the life of the church becomes a blur of pretty colors and nifty slogans and we are caught in a preoccupation with programs.

Regrettably, the more a congregation loses members, the more it seems to invest increasing amounts of leadership, time, and financial resources in more and more programs. It is as if local congregations seek to recover the busy, bustling days of programs of the churched culture of the 1950s. Those days are gone and done. We look forward to the mission field God now gives us.

The hope for congregations who seek to be strong and healthy in the mission culture of our time is to focus on people, not a plethora of programs. The good news is: your congregation can have this seventh central characteristic well in place by having one major program. It is no longer the number or quantity of programs. It is not a matter of busyness. It is a matter of having one major program.

The hope for our time is to be a people caring congregation, not a program-driven church. The hope is not in program development and program coordination. We quit seeking to offer everything and anything for everybody all the time. We overextend our resources and end up creating the mediocre middle. Our hope is in carrying out one major program so well that the congregation develops a community-wide respect for the competence of this one program.

The congregation becomes increasingly effective and successful. Strength breeds strength. Success breeds success. With spillover impact, this major program nurtures the gifts, strengths, and competencies of people in the congregation. We know that the purpose of our one major program is people, not program. With our one major program well in place, *people are helped . . . . hope is shared . . . . grace is given.*

Rating Guide: One Major Program

Item	Maximum Points	Our Congregation's Rating
1. We have one major program that is among the best in the community.	25	_____
2. Our one major program serves many persons and families.	25	_____
3. The leaders of this program are both person centered and program centered.	25	_____
4. Our one major program has some connection with our one major mission outreach.	25	_____
Total	100	_____

Instructions

- Use the resources of this chapter to evaluate your congregation's rating in each of the listed items.
- Enter your rating numbers in the blanks. Then, find the total.
- Divide the total of your score by 10 to obtain your congregation's rating on a scale of 1 to 10.
- Enter your rating of One Major Program on the chart in Appendix C on page 258.

Further Resources

The Future That Has Come
Twelve Keys for Living
Effective Church Leadership
The Twelve Keys Bible Study

8

OPEN ACCESSIBILITY

Mark said, "I know the church is somewhere right around here. They told us, when I called the church office, to turn right on Green, left on Maple, left on Wadsworth, left on Sidney, go three blocks, and we would see the church. I do not see the church. We have followed the directions twice."

Ethel said, "We will be late for the wedding. It is almost time. Call the church."

Mark phoned. "There is no answer. We can leave a message. They will get back to us on Monday."

"This is Saturday. You would think someone would be there because of the wedding. Let's ask that man in his front yard," Ethel said.

The man said, when Mark and Ethel asked, "Yes, here is how you get to the church." He gave simple directions that made sense.

Then, he said, "I would be a very rich person if I had fifty cents for each time I have been asked for directions to that church. It is the most hard to find church I have ever seen. You are not alone. I have already had several cars stop me for directions, headed to the same wedding."

One key, one possibility, for a strong, healthy congregation is open accessibility.

A strong, healthy congregation

- Has an excellent location, matching with the traffic direction patterns and average trip time horizons of our community
- Has generous site accessibility with adequate points of ingress and egress to our site
- Offers open, spacious entrances and exits to our building and helpful visible and hidden signs of welcome
- Shares a "people accessibility" of compassion with members, constituents, persons served in mission, and community persons

Through open accessibility, people discover a congregation that shares the grace of God in their lives. Open accessibility is a gift of grace. People discover the accessibility of God's grace in their lives. People grow lives of grace.

LOCATION ACCESSIBILITY

Our congregation has an excellent location, matching with the traffic direction patterns and average trip time horizons of our community.

"Location, location, location." Solid business persons, excellent real estate developers, and gifted city planners are apt to say, "Three factors are important in developing a successful project or business. The first factor is location, the second factor is location, and the third factor is location." This key is a functional characteristic, and has an important value in developing a strong, healthy congregation.

Some congregations are home congregations. The basic principles apply. Whether the location is a home, a store front, a rented location, or one the congregation owns, open accessibility is helpful. Open accessibility includes the four factors listed above. All four help a congregation have the strength of open accessibility.

The first is location accessibility. Many congregations benefit by having a location that is accessible, sometimes on a major corner. Location accessibility includes two good friends: *traffic direction patterns and average trip times in the community.*

People tend to go to church in relation to their traffic direction patterns in day-to-day life. Congregations on multiple traffic direction patterns have more possibilities to serve persons. They have a strong capacity to help people with their lives and destinies. A helpful location is on several of these traffic direction patterns of people, as they move about the community:

> going to work
> major shopping
> school activities
> major social and recreational activities

You can think of location with this spirit.

an excellent location	matches with all four traffic direction patterns
a solid location	matches with two to three of the traffic patterns
a fragile location	matches with one traffic direction pattern
a difficult location	does not match with any traffic direction pattern

Some congregations plan to be large, regional congregations, serving a major area of people. It is important that the location match with three or four of the major traffic direction patterns. Some congregations plan to be small, strong congregations. It is likewise helpful for the location to match with three or four of the major traffic direction patterns. They will be better able to be small and strong in an excellent location.

Some congregations have located on a site that resonates with the school traffic pattern. This works well so long as the congregation has the ability to focus on the children and the families of that school. Sometimes, the education district closes the school. We are now in a tough position, made even more difficult when the school and the church are located "inside" one subdivision. A more resilient location is to be on two or three major traffic patterns.

When people travel from north to the south going to work, to major shopping, to major schools, and to major social and recreational activities, the best site would be one on the north-to-south pattern of traffic. People find it natural to travel to that church location. It is concurrent with their traffic direction patterns in day-to-day life.

They are more likely to travel fifteen to twenty-five minutes along their day-to-day traffic pattern to that church location. They are less likely to turn in the opposite direction of their normal patterns to travel ten minutes to attend a church. People are more likely to travel to a church site that is located in harmony with their normal traffic direction patterns.

Location accessibility and average trip time are good friends. The best site takes seriously the average trip time in the community. People measure trips in minutes, not miles. We ask how far it is to the nearest shopping center. The answer comes, "It is about fifteen minutes." "How far is it in miles?" "I told you, it is fifteen minutes." People think more in time, not distance, minutes, not miles.

People have regular patterns of average trip time. They develop a trip time horizon. In some communities, the average trip time horizon is twenty-five minutes. In other communities, the average trip time is fifteen minutes. Think of the current average trip time in your community. Think of what the average trip time is projected to be over the coming ten years. In some instances, congregations will benefit because, over the years to come, the average trip time may grow longer, simply due to traffic congestion. It will take longer to go the same distance.

People tend to drive their average trip time horizon. People tend to invest approximately the same amount of time traveling to church that they invest in an average trip during the course of the week—an average trip to work, to do major shopping, to school, or to participate in social and recreational activities.

Some locations matched the traffic direction patterns and average trip times of the community fifty to ninety years ago. In the course of time, a new main road was developed, in another part of the community. The traffic direction patterns shifted to the new main road. The average trip time patterns changed. Time passed. Over the years, as people's habits shifted to the new main road, these congregations lost their original location accessibility.

Some congregations never had location accessibility. Their location was a bargain. The developer was *kind* and gave the land to the church. It was on the back side of the large subdivision. There is a large drainage ditch, running diagonally through the church property. With a heavy rain, the ditch would fill as it drained away the water from the whole subdivision. The developer could not use the property for housing. It was too expensive to install large drainage culverts and cover the ditch. He gave the property to the new church.

The congregation was creative. They put their parking on one side of the drainage ditch, the side nearest to the road. They built their facilities on the back side of the drainage ditch. They built a pass-over, walking bridge over the drainage ditch. People would park on one side, cross over the walking bridge, and share worship and Sunday School on the other side.

Yet, even as the land had been free, the primary problem continued to harm them. It was a poor location. It was not accessible. No one could find the church. It was on the back side of the subdivision. No one drove in that direction. The entrance and exit to the subdivision were in the opposite direction. Here, Lewis and Clark would take two years to find it. It had no accessibility. It had no visibility. In time, the congregation moved to a stronger location.

Some locations are visible but no one can find how to get to them.

You and I are having fun. We are headed to a specific church location. It is on a main road. We have driven by the location many times. It is highly visible. The church location is on a six-lane highway, with three lanes going each way. Many people see this location each day. The church location is in the middle of a long stretch of this main road. To the east, about a half of a mile, is one intersection. To the west, about the same distance, is another intersection.

You and I exit at the east intersection. We drive north several blocks. We turn left into the subdivision where the church is located. We encounter streets that twist and turn, curve and curl, meander and circle, with no discernable pattern. Yes, here it would take Lewis and Clark more than two years to find the church. The church has no open accessibility to its location.

People go to the church nearest their heart, not their house. They invest their average trip time doing so. They have found home with this congregation. Sometimes, they drive longer, when their heart is deeply touched. Traffic direction patterns and average trip time contribute to location accessibility.

SITE ACCESSIBILITY

We have generous site accessibility with adequate points of ingress and egress to our site.

The site has a sense of openness. The more open and spacious the site, the more likely people are to experience the site as accessible. The more closed in and cluttered the site, the more likely people are to sense inaccessibility. People are drawn to open, not closed, locations. They are drawn to spacious, not cluttered and crowded locations.

Landscaping helps. We will share more on landscaping in Key Ten. For now, it is helpful to confirm that landscaping communicates openness and spaciousness. A site with a large building built right up to the street will feel less open and less accessible than a site where the building is set back from the street with sufficient green space, landscaping, and parking surrounding it. The interrelationship of land, landscaping, and parking contributes to this sense of openness. The architectural design of the buildings contributes. Some locations "feel" more open than others.

This site is easy to enter and leave. The technical terms are ingress and egress. The larger the site, the more important it is to have multiple entrances and exits. The smaller the site, the easier it is to get by with only one or two ways of entering and leaving. A common mistake is to select a large piece of property, then to provide only one point for entering and leaving the property. Such an arrangement seriously hinders the site accessibility.

Entrances and exits to the property are best designed for two lanes of traffic at each point. Less desirable are one-lane, one-way entrances and exits. In larger sites, it is important to have three traffic lanes at each point of entry: one for entry, one for exit, and one for left-hand turns. Consider the volume, the size of the traffic flow on your ten major Sundays.

Many congregations benefit by having more than one service of worship. When this is so, we help with the "turnover time" between worship services. Some people who are coming to the next service have already come, while some people who are leaving the first service have not yet left. It is excellent that we have more than one service, and we will want to have generous ingress and egress for this turnover time. Look wisely at the ingress and the egress dynamics of your site on your ten best Sundays of the year. Include Christmas Eve, Christmas, and Easter.

BUILDING ACCESSIBILITY

The building offers open, spacious entrances and exits to our building and helpful visible and hidden signs of welcome.

The building offers accessible entrances and exits. Too few churches have built facilities with adequate attention to this.

A building that has entrances with large vestibule areas at the major entrances and exits is most helpful.

The larger the congregation, the more important it is to have more than one major entrance. It is useful to have a major entrance near the "real front door." The real front door is the door nearest the parking. People park their car and head to the nearest door. Some congregations have a "street-side" front door with a major entrance and welcoming area. The parking is "in the back."

The "real front door" is the single, thirty-inch-wide door at the back, nearest the parking. Thus, we wisely have a second major entrance nearest the parking. The front entrance is the "curb-side appeal" entrance. In good weather, some people may park and walk around the building to that distant "curbside appeal" door. Mostly, people head to the door nearest to where they have parked. Feel free to have more than one spacious entrance.

Our major entrances are generous in providing accessibility for persons with handicapping conditions. We provide ease of accessibility at one of our major entrances, adjacent to adequate parking. There are no curbs between the car parking spaces and the door. If a ramp is helpful, it is of a gentle slope, wide, with handrails.

We offer visible and "hidden" signs that communicate a sense of openness, warmth, and accessibility . . . . of welcome and invitation. First-time worshipers feel welcomed by what they see. There are no hidden signs that flash, "Proceed with Caution" or "Handicapped Persons Not Welcome." Some congregations, regrettably, have a hidden sign that says, "Guess Where the Sanctuary Is; We Know, and We Aren't Telling." Some churches hang out the hidden sign, "We Know Where the Parking Is; We Have Our Parking Space; You Figure Out What to Do."

With many congregations, the site location itself is indeed accessible. But the congregation, unwittingly, hangs out enough hidden signs that communicate closedness, barriers, and inaccessibility. They communicate closed, cliquish, clannish, and exclusive. People conclude that the location, the site, the buildings, and the congregation are not accessible.

Fortunately, many congregations have buildings that communicate open accessibility. They have entrances and exits that are accessible. With visible and hidden signs they communicate a spirit of open, warm, welcome, and inclusive.

A generous sense of openness, adequate entering and leaving the property, spacious entrances and exits to the buildings, and "hidden signs" that share openness, warmth, and welcome all contribute to helpful site accessibility.

PEOPLE ACCESSIBILITY

Our congregation shares a "people accessibility" of compassion with members, constituents, persons served in mission, and community persons.

Open accessibility is the result of location accessibility, site accessibility, building accessibility, *and* people accessibility. Together, these four help a congregation to be strong and healthy.

People accessibility includes the spirit of open accessibility that the congregation has with these four groupings . . . .

one another	many congregations share an open spirit across the whole congregation and a genuine sense of family together
her shepherding leaders	they have an open spirit of sharing and caring, compassion, and community with one another
her pastor and staff	together, they encourage and practice a spirit of people accessibility
persons in the community	there is a spirit of people accessibility, of genuine respect, and of compassion with persons in the community

Many congregations are open, warm, welcoming, and inclusive with all four of these groupings. These are strong, healthy congregations. Sometimes, a congregation is strong and healthy, and this creates a spirit of people accessibility. Sometimes, the spirit of people accessibility helps a congregation to be strong and healthy. Each dynamic helps the other.

Some congregations are open, warm, welcoming, and inclusive with two or three of these four "groupings." They will tend toward being weak, declining congregations. Some congregations are open, warm, welcoming, and inclusive with one of these "groupings." They will be nearly dying congregations. Some congregations have decided to be closed, cliquish, clannish, and exclusive. They have decided to die or are already almost dead.

Some congregations are tenuous about their own internal relationships. They "huddle up." They fear being open with other people. They worry that their own tenuous, near-collapse relationships will, in fact, collapse. It is not that they close up because they are secure in their relationships. It is the opposite. The fragile nature of their relationships creates anxiety and fear. They have all they can say grace over to *almost* get along with one another. It is about all they can do to get along with one another. They do not have the confidence and energy to be open with new persons. Their people accessibility is zero.

Most persons discern the warmth, the people accessibility of a whole congregation by their contacts with specific individuals in the congregation. This is how they assess, with some degree of reliability, how much people accessibility there is within a congregation. Intuitively, they listen and look for a series of clues as to the strength of the people accessibility.

They discover that several people speak to them, warmly, when they come to worship. They sense that the key leaders and the pastor have an open-door spirit. They are welcome. They discern that the key leaders have open, invitational meetings, not closed, secret meetings. Information is generously shared. Shepherding is of considerable depth. People experience a spirit of openness and caring, compassion and sharing, community and family.

They experience the pastor and key leaders investing time in informal conversations with persons in the congregation and community. By contrast, some pastors and key leaders are so busy with formal meetings and projects that there is not sufficient open time for them to share in informal conversations. The ease with which the key leaders and pastor can be reached in times of emergency, illness, and death is a further clue as to how much people accessibility there is.

People accessibility includes accessibility with the community. Key leaders, grassroots members, pastor, and staff participate directly in some of the worthwhile groupings and projects of the community. The more they contribute to some key activities within the community, the more that community people feel this congregation has strong people accessibility.

A congregation may not have location, site, or building accessibility. We can compensate for the lack of these by developing a strong, generous practice of people accessibility. We can accomplish this through shepherding visitation or one, major, helpful, legendary mission outreach in the community, or both. The first or second characteristics of strong, healthy congregations can help with the eighth, open accessibility.

The community grapevine has considerable speed.

The word spreads quickly about a congregation's people accessibility. The pastor and the key leaders are accessible to persons in the community. The community at large is grateful. This is especially so when the congregation serves persons in the community with one, helpful, legendary mission outreach.

A congregation delivers its one, major, compelling, helpful mission in the community, not inside the church. The mission is effective and helpful. The congregation becomes a legend on the community grapevine for helpfulness with people. One congregation developed an extraordinary missional outreach with alcoholics and their families. This congregation delivers one of the most competent and effective missional approaches with alcoholics and their families in the country. They have an *inaccessible* location. They have a most *accessible* mission.

Many congregations share increasingly helpful shepherding visitation. The less accessible the location is . . . . the more important shepherding becomes. The site may be inaccessible. Thus, we can be accessible in the community gathering events, in places of work, in recreational gatherings, and in people's homes.

We advance our shepherding accessibility. We strengthen persons in their lives. The happy by-product is that the key of open accessibility is also advanced. We counter, we overcome a lack of location, site, and building accessibility by creating a strong sense of people accessibility. This is a happy by-product of shepherding visitation.

I encourage congregations to look at one, major, helpful, legendary mission and shepherding visitation as ways of improving and enhancing open accessibility. During the coming years, open accessibility will become increasingly important. The more crowded and cluttered our towns and cities become, the more important open accessibility will become. The more complex and difficult our lives become, the more important that congregations be accessible and open.

Your congregation can grow an intentional, encouraging, assertive accessibility. You can develop one or more of these four: location accessibility, site accessibility, building accessibility, or people accessibility. You will help persons with their lives and destinies.

Rating Guide: Open Accessibility

Item	Maximum Points	Our Congregation's Rating
1. We have an excellent location, matching with the traffic direction patterns and average trip time horizons of our community.	25	_____
2. We have generous site accessibility with adequate points of ingress and egress to our site.	25	_____
3. We offer open, spacious entrances and exits to our building and helpful visible and hidden signs of welcome.	25	_____
4. We share a "people accessibility" of compassion with members, constituents, persons served in mission, and community persons.	25	_____
Total	100	_____

Instructions

- Use the resources of this chapter to evaluate your congregation's rating in each of the listed items.
- Enter your rating numbers in the blanks. Then, find the total.
- Divide the total of your score by 10 to obtain your congregation's rating on a scale of 1 to 10.
- Enter your rating of Open Accessibility on the chart in Appendix C on page 258.

Further Resources

Building for Effective Mission
The Future That Has Come
The Twelve Keys Bible Study

9

HIGH VISIBILITY

———

Dorothy said to Wil, "Where did that church come from? I don't think I have seen that church before. Look at the flowers someone has planted out front."

Dorothy and Wil later told me of their conversation in the car that day. They shared that they had driven by the church countless times. It was on Wil's way to work. It was on Dorothy's way to visit her best friend. They had never "seen" the church until that day.

Time passed.

The three new flower beds they had first noticed became five beds of warm, attractive flowers. The flowers were well done and well cared for. Dorothy and Wil began to think of the church as "the church where the flowers are."

They went on to say, "When our son was in the hospital, victim of a hit-and-run driver, we did not know who to call. We found the name of the church, called the pastor, and asked if he would come. He did. This is our church now."

One key, one possibility, for a strong, healthy congregation is high visibility.

A strong, healthy congregation:

- Has excellent site visibility of its church location
- Has helpful signs and seasonal points of interest, which give it high visibility

- Has excellent communications visibility with the congregation and the community
- Has excellent people visibility in a worthwhile community project

It is hard for the leaders and pastor of a congregation to see the church and its corresponding visibility as it is seen by persons in the community. A vast number of leaders and pastors mistakenly assume that the way they see the church is the way everyone sees it. Their own familiarity with the church gets in the way.

High visibility allows us an opportunity to invite people to share God's grace. Community persons are more likely to share in God's grace when we are positively visible to them.

SITE VISIBILITY

Our congregation has excellent site visibility of our church location.

It is straightforward. Some church sites can be seen. Some cannot be seen. Occasionally, the site's visibility is marginal. You can assess the visibility of a given church site by considering:

many people drive by the church site each day
the church site can be easily seen from one or more major streets or roads
the site has an open, spacious appearance

When their longing for the grace of God stirs them, many persons go to the church that they have "seen" on their traffic direction patterns. They have driven by the church. Community persons tend not to know what denominations are. They do not look in the yellow pages for the nearest church of a given denomination. They are drawn to a congregation (1) that they have seen as they travel around the community, or (2) that is a legend on the community grapevine for a specific mission outreach.

The more people who see a given church site, the more likely some of them are to think of that congregation as a possible source of grace and help.

One factor is "high side of the road" visibility. If we are searching for a new location, either for a new congregation or to relocate a current congregation, we would secure property on the high side of major roads. Locations on the "low side" of the road, "down in the gulley," are virtually invisible. It may be one thing to *sing* about the church in the valley. It is quite another thing for churches to be located on the low side of the road so they are hardly seen.

Regrettably, some groups settle for a piece of property on the low side of the road because they think it will be cheaper. The initial cost of the property is less. It is precisely because it is on the low side of the road that it costs so much less. But the price that is paid over the coming forty to sixty to a hundred years of that congregation's existence is not worth the initial savings. High-side visibility is important to the physical visibility of the site.

We are not wanting a site on the "high, high side of the road." Such sites are so high up and elevated that people have to crane their necks to look up through the windshield of their cars to "almost" see the site. A cliff-side site is less helpful. What we are looking for is a site that has a reasonable "angle of the neck" view of the site as we drive by.

Another factor of physical visibility is the amount of frontage on the road or roads adjacent to the property. Again, some groups occasionally select a site that may contain as much as five to seven to ten acres, but the frontage on the major road is no more than fifty to a hundred feet. This slim corridor of land leads back to the larger acreage. But the site is hidden by other buildings on adjacent land on either side of the thin lane to the congregation's property. The narrower the frontage, the less visible the site will be, no matter how many acres it may contain.

Site visibility is enhanced by extensive frontage on the principal roads adjacent to the property.

Every road has a "speed of the traffic" dynamic. There is a correlation between the speed limit and the speed of the traffic. As people drive by, they have "x" amount of time to view a site. The faster the speed, the less time they have. A narrow frontage provides minimal time to "see" the site. A stronger frontage allows more time to actually see the church site.

SIGNS AND POINTS OF INTEREST VISIBILITY

Our congregation has helpful signs and seasonal points of interest, which give us high visibility.

Church signs take seriously the speed of the traffic passing by. The faster the speed, the briefer the sign. A sign matches the speed of the traffic. When the speed of the traffic is thirty-five miles per hour, have on the sign only as much information as one can read in a two-second glance. Think of the speed of the traffic, not the speed limit. There is no necessary correlation.

The sign that takes six seconds to read has too much information. This is a sign from a walking culture. We used to read the sign walking by, on our way to the town square. Wherever we have a walking culture, such a sign works. Some neighborhood congregations are in "walking" subdivisions. Have a "walking" sign. We do have many signs left over as archaeological relics of that long-ago walking culture, and they are now located in a driving culture.

A driver glances at a sign. The driver sees that he or she *can* read the sign in the time available for their glance. They read the sign. A driver glances at a sign. The driver sees that she or he *cannot* read the full sign in the time they have available. They do not read the sign. When a person cannot read the whole sign, they tend to not read any of the sign. The sign has too much clutter and is too crowded. Drivers have more important things to do—like keeping their cars on the road—than to try to read all the information.

Signs do not need to have the words, "Visitors Are Welcome." The shape of the sign, the position of the sign, the colors used for background, and the lettering will all communicate a sense of warmth and welcome. A nearby "point of interest" such as a patch of flowers that has beauty and color will communicate a sense of welcome.

Some signs are put up by persons who already know what congregation it is. They match the sign to the building. The sign is parallel to the building and the road. Some are perpendicular. Both types of signs match the building and road. They may or may not match the people.

Drive the speed of the traffic on the "going to work" side of the road. Find the longest line of sight through the windshield of a car. Place a sign that matches this longest line of sight visibility. Drive the speed of the traffic on the "going to home" side of the road. Place another sign that matches this longest line of sight visibility. Some communities have sign regulations. As best we can, we match the longest lines of sight visibility for people passing the church site.

The faster the speed of the traffic, the more important it is to match the signs with an adequate line of sight. Drivers read the sign from some distance away rather than trying to catch a sign parallel or perpendicular to the church at the very point at which they are passing both the sign and the church. Any parallel or perpendicular sign that has stood for years faithfully in front of our church building can be left in place. We add new signs to advance our visibility.

Signs match the community the congregation seeks to serve. Signs use words, colors, textures, shapes, and lettering that match the vocational, life stage, common interests, and sociological groupings the congregation is serving and looks forward to serving. Signs are tasteful and artfully done. They look attractive. The signs match the mission more than the mortar. In my travels across the planet as a speaker and consultant, I have seen a vast variety of signs that congregations have done. Most are well done.

The physical visibility of a church site can be improved as we develop special event signs and modest "points of interest." We can post attractive, interesting signs that highlight special events happening at the church, for example, for Christmas Eve, Easter, Vacation Bible School. These help persons see our site in fresh, new ways.

Churches that fail to add "points of interest" to their landscaping from one year to the next tend to become anonymous buildings. People pass by but do not really see them. Shrubbery and trees are allowed to grow tall and bushy. They "overgrow" the site. They interfere with the essential view of the site and the building. As time passes, the church site becomes increasingly invisible.

In our landscaping, we can change one or two points of interest each year. People see the site in fresh, new ways. "Oh, where did that church come from?" people ask. In the front yard, one or two modest flower beds can create points of interest. We can advance the size and shape and color of these flower beds from one year to the next. We can move the spot from time to time.

These modest points of interest will catch the attention of community persons.

COMMUNICATIONS VISIBILITY

Our congregation has excellent communications visibility with the congregation and the community.

Communications visibility happens with Web site, postal service, e-mail, cell phone, text message, newspaper, and social networking opportunities. It also happens with radio and television. Many congregations are advancing their visibility through many of these methods. They use these resources to contribute to the high visibility of their congregation.

Jesus said, "Let your light so shine before people, that they may see your good works and give glory to your Father who is in heaven." We are encouraged to share good news of good works, of the concrete ways in which people's lives and destinies are being touched with the grace of God. We are encouraged to give glory to God.

There is nothing that suggests we lift up a litany of busy, bustling, merry-go-round programs, activities, and committee meetings. There is nothing that suggests we take credit for what God is doing in people's lives. The spirit of the text is joy for the grace of God and gratitude that God is moving, stirring, and working in the lives and destinies of persons. We give glory to God.

Sometimes, we feel uncomfortable about communications visibility. We fear "blowing our own horn." We begin to think this is something with which we should not be involved. Then, we come to realize that every grouping or organization, to a greater or lesser extent, is discussed in the community. Thus, we share an active program of communications visibility . . . . with integrity.

Integrity is the first element in communications. Many congregations share communications with a spirit of honesty and integrity. Precisely because they share with integrity, people listen to what they are sharing. People are astute at discerning communications that have integrity, substance, and strength.

Content is the second element in communications. We share, with integrity, the content of what we are doing. With grace and compassion, we share about our mission with persons in the community and beyond. A few churches focus on what people can do for that church. Their "pitch" is on trying to get people to come and volunteer in that church's programs and activities.

Some content focuses on high-powered promises of what that church can do for them. People are not looking for a kind of chocolate syrup poured over flavorless ice cream to make it taste sweet. Most people are not interested in overstatements about what a church can do for them. They are interested in knowing what the church is doing to be of help in the community so that the community will be a better place in which to live.

John sent his disciples to Jesus with the question, "Are you the one to come or should we look for another?" The answer was not, "Documents are being drafted, reports are being drawn up, meetings are being held, and see, all the efforts we are making to become bigger." The answer was, "Look, the blind see, the lame walk, the naked are being clothed, the Gospel is being shared with the poor." Concrete acts of help are happening now. It is not that something may happen or will happen in the future. Acts of grace are happening now.

Trust is the third element in communications. The congregation develops a spirit of trust with the community and with the media groupings in the community. This includes a mutual trust with the various grapevine grouping networks. Word travels fast on the grapevine. When there is no trust, the grapevine becomes the graveyard. When there is mutual trust and respect, the grapevine helps us live forward to a better day.

PEOPLE VISIBILITY

Our congregation has excellent people visibility in a worthwhile community project.

The best signs are people. People point people to a congregation. People who are visible in a worthwhile project in the community contribute to the visibility of a congregation. Mostly, these persons are quiet and modest. They have humility. They are shy of publicity. They do their mission work with the hope that their help will be effective. They do not want publicity. They do not want their work to be ballyhooed abroad.

These persons are saints. Not sought, they have the visibility of being significantly helpful in the lives of people. The grapevine knows of their gifts of grace. The more persons the congregation has helping in the community, not in the church, the more the congregation will have visibility in the community. This is because of what persons do, not because of what they say.

People visibility is as important as site visibility, signs and points of interest visibility, and communications visibility. Indeed, the less the site visibility of the location, the *more* important it is that there is strong people visibility in the community. People visibility means that some of the key leaders, some of the grass-roots, and the pastor and staff of a congregation are involved in a worthwhile project in the community. It is not that they participate in a broad range of community activities. Rather, they participate well and fully in one, maybe two.

The community grapevine has a good feeling about a congregation's life and work. The grapevine senses that this congregation has created a solid practice of helping people. In some instances, a congregation is virtually a living legend on the community grapevine. When this happens, the congregation has an extraordinarily high degree of people visibility.

The important factor in grapevine visibility is the character and content of what is communicated. Congregations with people visibility tend to have the kind of visibility that identifies the congregation as a source of help, home, and hope . . . . as a source of confidence and assurance, reliability and certainty amidst the difficulties and transitions of everyday life.

A congregation need not develop a preoccupation with people visibility. One can "overcome" a lack of open accessibility or a lack of high visibility by delivering two of the first four of the *Twelve Keys*—mission, shepherding, worship, or groupings. The more well in place two of these four, the higher the level of satisfaction in a congregation.

At the same time, a helpful combination is to have both open accessibility and high visibility. These two are good friends. They reinforce one another. Some congregations have open accessibility and no visibility. Some congregations have high visibility but suffer a lack of accessibility. Wherever possible, it is helpful for a congregation to have both well in place.

Rating Guide: High Visibility

Item	Maximum Points	Our Congregation's Rating
1. We have excellent site visibility of our church location.	25	_____
2. Our helpful signs and seasonal points of interest give us high visibility.	25	_____
3. We have excellent communications visibility with the congregation and the community.	25	_____
4. We have excellent people visibility in a worthwhile community project.	25	_____
	_____	_____
Total	100	_____

Instructions

- Use the resources of this chapter to evaluate your congregation's rating in each of the listed items.
- Enter your rating numbers in the blanks. Then, find the total.
- Divide the total of your score by 10 to obtain your congregation's rating on a scale of 1 to 10.
- Enter your rating of High Visibility on the chart in Appendix C on page 258.

Further Resources

Building for Effective Mission
The Future That Has Come
The Twelve Keys Bible Study

10

LAND, LANDSCAPING, AND PARKING

We were running ten minutes late.

I could not find my shoes. I finally found the car keys. Then, I found my glasses. We were walking out the door. Late. The phone rang. It was Aunt Wilda. We talked briefly.

Then, we were on our way. Fifteen minutes late. I made up five minutes. We were now ten minutes late. In thirty years of going to my church, I had never been late.

I pulled into the parking lot and made my usual right turn to my own parking space. I have parked in that same place for thirty years. I have sat in the same pew for the same number of years. I have filed deeds on both at the nearby county courthouse. Everyone knows where I park and where I sit. Most other leaders have their own parking space and pew as well.

Someone was pulling into my parking space.

A new blue SUV. Who has the nerve to park in my space? I started to honk my horn.

Just as I began to press down, my son got out of the car. I had forgotten they had just bought a new car. I started

to ask him to move his car. I remembered he had ridden
with his mother and me to church, and as a child and
youth, as a passenger in our family car, he was familiar
with that same space.

Fortunately, I was slow to say anything.

Our three grandchildren climbed out of the back seats.
They saw me. "Grandpa, we are coming to church with
you." They ran to my car. I got out. I hugged each one.
They bubbled with joy and love. They ran around to the
other side of the car to hug their grandmother. They were
so excited. "We are going to church with you," they sang
with joy, bouncing up and down.

I said to my son, "Your mother and I will be right in.
Glad we can worship together as family this morning."

As my wife and I parked in a distant space and walked
to the church, I said to her, "Phyllis, we are going to
help the church buy that lot next door. This is a normal
Sunday. The parking is virtually full. We can plan on helping our grandchildren worship with us. We'll buy the lot
and give it to the church."

And they did.

One key, one possibility, for a strong, healthy congregation is
land, landscaping, and parking.
   A strong, healthy congregation:

- Owns sufficient, usable land for our present life and future
  mission
- Has landscaping that contributes to a first impression of an
  open and spacious, warm and welcoming, inviting and gracious spirit
- Has adequate parking for our ten major Sundays of the year

- Has adequate parking for our normal Sundays and for our weekday use

It is hard for the leaders and pastor of a congregation to see the church and its land, landscaping, and parking as it is seen by persons in the community. A vast number of leaders and pastors mistakenly assume that the way they see the church is the way everyone sees it. Their own familiarity with the church gets in the way.

Adequate land, landscaping, and parking allow us an opportunity to invite people to God's grace. Community persons are more likely to share in God's grace when we positively welcome them.

LAND

Our congregation owns sufficient, usable land for our present life and future mission.

Many congregations across the planet do not own land. They are small, strong congregations. They gather in homes. They share, borrow, rent, or lease a land site and space for their life together. Countless congregations gather for mission, shepherding, worship, and community without owning land.

Many families live in one location, in one house, for a time. Then, they move to another house. Time passes. They move to yet another house. Congregations do the same. Over a fifty- to hundred-year period, many congregations have moved from one site to another. We located on the original site in 1868. We moved to a new site in 1921. We moved to another new newest site in 1948. We have been at our present site since 2001.

When we think of land, we think ten to thirty to fifty to one hundred years ahead. As someone wisely said, "They are not making any more land. Oh, maybe on some island in the Pacific they are, but not around here." Whenever we have the opportunity to improve our land position, I encourage many congregations to do so.

A piece of property comes on the market, or we hear that it may be coming on the market soon. We would benefit from having it. We do not wait too long to secure it. We can secure it with an option to purchase, a first right of refusal, or a purchase contract proposal. When it is gone, it is gone.

I encourage congregations to have an ongoing "land study team." This team of three persons, trusted and knowledgeable, is authorized to negotiate a contract with the owner of a piece of land or a building. They secure the owner's signature on a contract. Then, they bring the matter to the congregation for conversation and approval.

There is nothing that prevents an owner of land from signing a contract. All contracts have a reasonable closing date and, importantly, a standard contingency clause that says "subject to financing." With the contract signed by the owner of the property, the congregation can then decide to purchase or not purchase the property. All contracts have this same standard contingency clause.

More congregations lose the chance for the piece of property that would benefit them because they have premature, open, sometimes heated, public discussions about the property, assuming no one in the wider community is listening.

In those public discussions, someone usually says, "I can remember the time when we could have bought that property for $_____." Yes, that was just shortly after the pilgrims landed at Plymouth Rock. Someone says something that either raises the price beyond reason, or, more often, offends the property owner. He or she decides they will never sell to the congregation.

We have a wise, thoughtful land study team. The team secures a solid contract proposal. The team negotiates a fair and reasonable price for the property, fair for the owner and fair for us. We look ten to thirty to fifty or more years ahead. We seek to have adequate land for our congregation and our mission.

Many congregations lack the land they need to deliver their mission. They do the best they can with the land they have. Sometimes, we are able to acquire adjoining, contiguous land to improve our ability to deliver our mission. Sometimes, we acquire additional land nearby, within a reasonable travel time and distance. In effect, we are one congregation with two sites.

Years and years ago, I was helping a congregation in a county seat town. We wanted to advance our mission with children and their families. The church site was on the town square. There was no land, or even adjacent, contiguous buildings, we could acquire.

We found ten acres fifteen minutes away and built a community life center for family activities and classrooms for preschool, after school, and Sunday School. The sanctuary on the town square, built in the late 1800s, is a magnificent worship space with wondrous stained glass windows. The congregation has benefited from its two sites for mission in the many years come and gone.

For the present, consider the land you now have. With wisdom, judgment, vision, common sense, and prayer, think of how adequate the land is for the strength and health of your congregation. Consider what amount of land is useful and helpful for your congregation.

In a metropolitan area, were we a small, strong congregation, our site might contain a modest amount of land, or as much as one acre, and sometimes, as many as five acres. For a healthy middle congregation, we might have five to seven acres. A large, regional congregation may benefit from having eight to twenty acres, depending on the nature of their mission. Were we a mega congregation, we may have twenty to eighty or more acres.

In county seat towns, villages, and rural areas, the amount of land that is adequate varies from the suggestions above. Mostly, strong, healthy congregations in these communities benefit from having one to three to eight acres of land. This depends on the long-term usage the congregation envisions for its property. A strong mission in recreation frequently invites us to have eight acres plus.

These ranges for land are suggestive possibilities, not written in stone. Each situation is distinct. What guides us is the range of mission we look forward to sharing on the land. We do want a balance of land, landscaping, recreation areas, parking, and buildings. We will be at our best with sufficient land that the site feels open and spacious, warm and welcoming.

Sometimes, a congregation will be given a piece of land. The donor is interested in helping. The land looks adequate for now. The church is grateful for the contribution. At the time, no one assesses clearly all the ways in which they might want to utilize the property. Over the years, they slowly discover that the original piece of land they were given is not adequate.

The size of a congregation's land significantly influences the landscaping, the number of parking spaces, and the size and number of buildings that can be placed on the church site. Some congregations tend to lack sufficient land. This hampers their total life and mission. As best you can, develop sufficient land for your present life and future mission.

LANDSCAPING

Our congregation has landscaping that contributes to a first impression of an open and spacious, warm and welcoming, inviting and gracious spirit.

Many congregations have excellent landscaping. They benefit from landscaping that is open and spacious, warm and welcoming, inviting and gracious. They do border landscaping around their parking areas and their buildings. They use low-growing flowers and shrubs that do not overpower the buildings. The landscaping conveys a sense of safety and security, is attractive and well-kept.

The landscaping contributes greatly to the sense of welcome and invitation and the spirit of openness and spaciousness. Passersby form their impression of the congregation by what they see as they drive past. Should they see crowded and cluttered landscaping, they are likely to be put off, to decide this congregation is not for them.

"You can never make a first impression a second time."
Many congregations do not realize the kind of impression they
make with their landscaping, with community persons even
more than their own church members. Sometimes, the landscaping communicates worn and tired, patchy and bedraggled,
faded and declining. We can deliver inviting landscaping, well
cared for and attractive.

We can deliver landscaping that matches with the family
we are. Likewise the landscaping can match with the persons and
families in the community we hope to reach. For example, we
have a mission with children and their families. The landscaping
has this mission spirit about it. We are not doing formal, styl-
ized gardens, with rigid, austere flower beds. Nor are we doing
shabby and neglected landscaping. We are doing more natural
types of landscaping similar to what we find around homes
with children living in them.

With landscaping, the art is to show something new each
year. It may be a new touch of flowers. It may be some new
low-growing shrubbery . . . . a touch. It may be a new sign. It
may be we replant a current bed with new and different flowers. We can dress an old building with excellent landscaping and
it becomes a new building.

Buildings disappear. Buildings become invisible. The more a
building stays the same out front . . . . year after year . . . . the more it
disappears. It recedes into the background. We drive by buildings every day of the week we do not "see." The art is to show
something new each year. People will notice the new flowers.
They will ask, "Where did that building come from?"

It is fun to be known as "the church that has the wonderful
flowers."

By contrast, some congregations communicate that they are
weak and declining by the fading and withering landscaping
out front. We do not fix all the landscaping up in one season.
We develop a three- to five-year landscaping plan. Some new
touch of landscaping shows up each year. We share who we
are . . . . who we are becoming with excellent landscaping.

Now, I help congregations, downtown, in central city areas, with a "lot line" building. There is no land with which to develop attractive landscaping. Here, we focus on the front of the building, the signage on the building, and on keeping our "front" clean and attractive. Sometimes, we do potted plantings. Sometimes, for safety and security reasons, we don't. We seek, as best we can, to create a helpful first impression.

These days, in many congregations, I discover generous givers who give an enduring gift to see to it that new flowers find their way, are planted, each year into the garden areas of the church site. Some congregations have identified three to four garden areas. Families have given an enduring gift to endow one of these garden areas in honor or memory of one or more persons. The annual budget mows the grass and sweeps the walks. The enduring gifts see that the garden areas are fresh and new, warm and inviting each year.

Even during the winter snows, we "see" the garden areas that have been and will come anew this spring. We are "the church where the flowers are."

OUR TEN BEST SUNDAYS

Our congregation has adequate parking for our ten major Sundays of the year.

Easter is God's way of teaching us our future. This is my way of saying that whatever is your biggest Sunday is God's way of teaching you the pool of persons who think of your congregation as home. Going to church is no longer "the thing to do" in this culture. It is not accidental that people are in worship in your congregation. They could have been in some other church. They could have been doing something else. Their presence and participation tells us that, if they had a church home, it is here with us.

Your strongest Sunday of attendance may be Christmas rather than Easter. It might be Christmas Eve. It could be Mother's Day.

Whatever the worship service, your strongest service is God's way of teaching you your present worship pool of persons.

The way forward is to develop your one major Sunday into two or three, and, eventually, over three to five years, into ten major community Sundays a year, including Easter, Christmas Eve, and Christmas. As you develop these ten major community Sundays, the happy by-product is that average worship attendance will grow. Community persons and occasional worshipers tend to come to major community Sundays; they find home; and they come more frequently.

My book ***Dynamic Worship*** has a helpful chapter that will benefit you.

Somewhere, in the second and third years of this process, we add adequate parking for "our major Sundays." The spillover impact on advancing our normal Sundays will be remarkable. Ten Sundays a year, we will be sharing stirring, helpful worship with the strength of "Easter and Christmas," and we will have adequate parking for these times.

We look, first, for whether we have adequate parking for our ten major Sundays.

"Dr. Callahan, we are grateful for your wisdom on the ***Twelve Keys.*** Your lecture is wonderful. We have benefited greatly from your suggestions on mission, shepherding, worship, and groupings. We came to your suggestions on land, landscaping, and parking, and we sort of chuckled. We want you to know we have very adequate parking."

I have heard this statement countless times. I respond this way: "Good friend, you have just taught me you are a key leader in your congregation." They look puzzled. I continue, "Key leaders come early. They help get things ready. They have their own parking space. They have their own pew. They have filed deeds on both at the nearby county courthouse. They even know who, as key leaders, parks where. "Oh, look, John and Betty have a new car."

Key leaders arrive early. The parking lot looks pretty empty. The same is true when they leave. Key leaders tend to things after worship is over. Most people have already gone. They see a nearly empty parking lot. We have plenty of parking.

The art is to go out during the first hymn of the worship service on your ten biggest Sundays of the year. Now, you are seeing your parking through the eyes of first-time worshipers, occasional worshipers, and community persons. Now, you are seeing it through the eyes of the many persons who do not have "their own parking space."

People will put up with inadequate parking two to three to four Sundays a year—Christmas, Easter, maybe two more . . . . sometimes as many as ten. They do not put up with inadequate parking forty Sundays a year. People do not put up with inadequate parking where they work, where they shop, or where they enjoy social and recreational activities. Oh, they will for a very special occasion, but not on a regular basis.

You and I are having fun. We are driving in a car. We are headed to lunch at a favorite restaurant we enjoy. We draw near. We see the parking lot is nearly full. We are celebrating a special occasion. We put up with the inadequate parking and squeeze our car into a remote space.

Many times, when we head to lunch, we are not celebrating a special occasion. We are simply having lunch. The lot of our favorite restaurant looks pretty full. We head on down the street to another restaurant where we know there is adequate parking. We will share good food, and have good fun.

The basic principle is this: people tend to go to church the same way they transport themselves to work, school, major shopping, and major social and recreational activities. In cultures where people transport themselves around on horseback, we talk about the number of hitching posts. In some parts of this country, people continue to transport themselves around with a horse and a buggy. Here we talk of adequate hitching rails and buggy space.

In cultures where people transport themselves around by mass transit, whether by trolley car, bus, subway, or some combination, we talk about our location being near the bus stop or the subway station. In cultures where people transport themselves around by walking, we talk of being on or near the primary walking paths. In cultures where people transport themselves around by car, we talk of parking spaces.

OUR NORMAL SUNDAYS AND WEEKDAY USE

Our congregation has adequate parking for our normal Sundays and for our weekday use.

Look for whether we have adequate parking for our ten major Sundays, for our normal Sundays, and for our weekday use. Regrettably, some congregations focus on having adequate parking for normal Sundays. They neglect having adequate parking for weekday use. They almost resign themselves to not having adequate parking on their ten major Sundays.

If you would like to have more Sundays that look like Easter and Christmas, then provide adequate parking for these major Sundays, and you will have more Sundays that look like Easter and Christmas.

Likewise, think of what will help with your normal Sundays and your weekday use. On your major Sundays, surrounding merchants and residents may understand your needs for parking. They may be less understanding on normal Sundays and through the week. Merchants and banks may count on using their own parking lots. Residents may decide they plan to park on the street in front of their own homes. The available parking may become restricted, be sharply diminished.

You can think of the occasions, through the week, when you want to have several large groupings of persons on your church site. More likely, think of the occasions when you want to have a variety of small groupings on your church site. Some congregations let their parking determine their program. The art is to shape your program to the people, not the parking.

It is helpful and important to consider two major factors:

Do we have adequate parking for our ten major Sundays of
   the year?
Do we have adequate parking for our normal Sundays and
   for our weekday use?

BASICS FOR PARKING

As you consider your parking for your ten major Sundays and
your normal Sundays and weekday use, three factors help:

parking, worship, giving
possibilities for parking
the value of your parking

Parking, Worship, Giving. There is a direct correlation between
parking and worship attendance. There is a direct correlation
between worship attendance and giving. The more adequate
the parking, the more likely there is to be strong participation
in worship. The stronger the participation in worship, the more
generous the giving. The three go together. The stronger the
parking, the stronger the attendance, the stronger the giving.

The church that is short on parking may very well be short
on worship attendance and, therefore, short on contributions.
People who worship in a congregation tend to contribute
to the congregation. People who are members of the congregation but who do not worship with us tend not to contribute
financially.

Some groups try to increase membership to increase
money. Members who do not worship with us do not give.
Persons who worship with us give. The art is to increase the
worship attendance, not the membership figure. Sometimes,
this means we increase the parking.

Take your ten best Sundays, including Christmas Eve, Christmas, and Easter. Count the cars. Count the people. Invite a team to count your cars in your parking lots, on the street, and in nearby business lots. Count all of the cars that have someone in worship or on-site with us at the same time. Think of the nursery, Sunday School classes, or other groups meeting at the same time as worship. When we have three worship services, we do the count for each service. Count all the people and all the cars that are present at the same time.

Divide. You will now have the number of persons per car per parking space. The consistent average usually turns out to be 1.75 persons per parking space. In an earlier time, in that long lost churched culture of a bygone era, the figure was four persons per car. Families had one car. In our time, a family of five drives two cars to church. When they have a teenager, they drive three cars.

I was helping one congregation. Years and years ago, the worship attendance was 400. They had one hundred parking spaces. Over the years come and gone, the worship attendance had declined to 170. Over the years, the strength of their shepherding, worship, and leadership had continued on an even keel. What was different was this: now, there were 1.75 persons per car, but they still had the same hundred parking spaces. I suggested we increase the parking. We did. Worship attendance increased. Giving increased.

Now, parking by itself will not increase worship attendance and giving. Inadequate parking is a source of dissatisfaction. Adequate parking is not a source of satisfaction; it lowers a source of dissatisfaction. It is simply that people have to put their car somewhere in order to worship with us.

Possibilities for Parking. Mostly, local congregations have available five kinds of parking:

> on-site parking, directly on the property of the congregation, adjacent to the main buildings of the church

nearby parking owned by the congregation, with full right
of use

off-street parking owned by someone else with whom
the congregation has a formal or informal agreement
to use it

off-street parking owned by someone else with whom
the congregation has *no* formal or informal agreement
to use it, but "borrows" its use, hoping for the best

on-street parking available for use by anyone

With regard to on-street parking, you can make a reasonable
judgment as to how many parking spaces are actually available
to you for worship and major activities. On the ten major
Sundays when you do your parking study, you can develop
some sense of this.

Some congregations make the mistake of counting *all* the
on-street parking spaces as though they would automatically
be available, especially on Sunday morning. This is not the case.
Residents may park on the street, in front of their homes. They
have the "silly" notion that it is all right for them to park in
front of their own home. Persons who participate in nearby
congregations may park on the street. Shoppers at nearby businesses may use on-street parking spaces.

I have found that a congregation is fortunate to be able to
count on 40 to 60 percent of the total on-street parking spaces
for its use on Sunday mornings. Certainly, there are scattered
exceptions to this across the country. The basic point is to be
realistic as to the number of on-street spaces available for your use.

It is important to be realistic as to the number of off-street
parking spaces available. I use the term "off-street" to designate
the parking spaces off the street that many churches depend
upon but that are not really owned by the church. I reserve
the term "on-site" for the parking that is directly owned by the
congregation.

Many congregations depend on the off-street parking available at adjacent banks, shops, or stores. Generally, various

businesses are willing for a local congregation to use their off-street parking on Sunday morning. Even if this is the case, it is useful for the congregation to ask seriously, "For how many years can we depend upon these nearby businesses to make their own off-street parking available to us?" I think of several banks whose insurance companies and lawyers have advised them to chain off their parking on the weekend so as to avoid any possibility of legal liability.

The most effective parking is on-site, near a main entrance, on the property owned by the congregation. The next most effective is somewhere on-site, near the building. The next most effective is off-street and on-street parking within one short walking block of the major space and facilities of the congregation.

Parking within a second block is less usable and desirable. It is doubtful if parking spaces three blocks away are useful. Sometimes, the only people who count those parking spaces are a few key leaders who already have their own "reserved" parking space near the main door. They do not walk the three blocks.

Consider the behavior patterns when people go to local shopping centers. Some individuals are three-minute individuals. They invest three minutes driving around the parking area looking for a space right next to the door so they will not have to walk very far. Some people are five-minute individuals. They invest five minutes in such a search. I even know of persons who will follow someone who is leaving the store loaded with packages, in the hopes that they will go to a car at one of the nearby spaces and drive away, thereby opening that space near the door.

Strong, healthy congregations are realistic about the amount of parking they have. They know the number of parking spaces they own. They are realistic about the number of off-street spaces available, that they do not own. They are realistic as to the number of on-street parking spaces they can count on Sunday after Sunday. They take seriously the factor that optimal parking is within the first short walking block.

The Value of Your Parking. Where a congregation is considering the purchase of additional property for parking, the helpful question is, "What is the value of the land to us?" The less
helpful way is to ask how much the land costs. A value-effective
approach calculates the amount of giving income we will
receive per new parking space each year, during the coming five
to eight to ten years and beyond.

In Appendix B, you will discover Chart B.2, "The Number
of Available Parking Spaces." This chart will help you to assess
the actual number of parking spaces available. Then, you will
discover Chart B.3, "The Annual Giving Value of Your Parking Spaces." This chart will help you assess the value of your
parking.

I was helping one congregation. The adjacent piece of
property had a selling price of $200,000. By research, analysis,
and the study of recent comparative land closings, it was deter-
mined this was a fair and reasonable price. We could place forty
new parking spaces on the piece of land. The congregation currently had one hundred parking spaces and a total annual giving
income of $300,000.

The average giving income per year for each current parking space is $3,000. To add forty new parking spaces would add
additional giving income of $120,000 per year. This is new giv-
ing income over five years of $600,000 compared with the pur-
chase price of $200,000 for the property. We might fill the forty
new parking spaces slowly. Ten new cars might park there in
year one. Twenty might do so in year two.

When it is reasonable to project the new parking will be
well used in the immediate years to come, and when we can
project that we will amortize our investment in five to eight to
ten years, we move forward and buy the land.

Frequently, someone thinks the owner has placed too high
a price on the property. They conclude it does not make sense
to purchase the land. The property is sold to another buyer.
The possibility of the church ever acquiring the land becomes
increasingly remote. This is not to suggest that the church

should buy a piece of land for whatever price someone asks. Rather, it is simply to confirm that a helpful way to proceed is to calculate the value of the new spaces in relation to the total net new giving income that we can project over a reasonable period of time.

Consider the "hidden sign" in front of your church. When the parking is full, it has the same discouraging effect as a sanctuary that is uncomfortably crowded. When the parking lot is full, the big hidden sign hung out front is "There Is No Room in the Inn for You." When there are some open parking spaces, the big hidden sign hung out front says "Come On In; There Is Room in the Inn for You."

WAYS TO HELP PARKING

Parking Greeters. One way to ease the parking is to establish a team of parking greeters who welcome persons, facilitate traffic flow, and extend help to people as they seek places to park. This is a major way to improve parking. The parking greeters deliver a major source of satisfaction amidst a source of dissatisfaction over inadequate parking.

Invite persons to serve as parking greeters who look friendly, have a warm personality, and some human relations skills. Parking greeters are trustworthy, reliable sources of help. They focus on welcoming persons, not "sternly directing traffic." They do take seriously the traffic flow patterns. They do make it easier for persons to enter and leave the church site.

In good weather, on a major Sunday, parking greeters may bring a card table, some Starbuck's coffee, orange juice, and donuts as a special treat. We began to develop an informal grouping for whom this parking lot feels like "home," like a warm, welcoming place.

You can have parking greeters who help on your ten major Sundays of the year. Some congregations have three parking greeter teams: a team that helps from late August through

Christmas, a team that helps from January through Easter, and a third team that helps from Easter through the summer.

The phrase is: "We can never make a first impression a second time." The landscaping, the parking, and the parking greeters are part of the "first impression" people have of us.

Multiple Services.   One way to ease the parking problem is to have more than one worship service. When we have two services of worship, we double our parking. When we have three services, we triple are parking. Now, technically, this does not quite double or triple parking spaces we have available, but multiple services do greatly improve the parking.

For example, at 9:30, we have both morning worship and church school. At 11:00, we have both worship and church school. Some persons come to 9:30 worship and go home. Some come to 9:30 worship, then go to church school at 11:00. Some persons come to 9:30 church school, then go to 11:00 worship. Some come to 11:00 worship.

There is the "turnover" time of 10:30 to 11:00, between services. We will want some turnover parking spaces for the people who are coming to the 11:00 service who have arrived before the people who are leaving at 10:30 have left.

Even with this factor, we will greatly increase our parking by having two services. We will advance our parking by having three services. The rule of thumb is: *the less parking we have, the more services we share.*

Stay and Go.   As we discussed earlier, one possibility is to stay at the present location and also develop a second campus. This solution helps both with the needed parking and with needed space and facilities. The congregation shares services of worship at both locations. Through the week, some activities occur at the main campus and some at the second campus.

Mission, Visitation, Worship, and Groupings.   One way to ease the parking problem is to develop effective strengths in two of these four: mission, visitation, worship, and groupings. People are more willing to put up with inadequate parking because of:

one, major, helpful legendary mission outreach the congregation shares in the community

shepherding visitation that persons experience in their lives, encouraging, restoring, and strengthening them, their family, and their friends

stirring, inspiring services of worship that touch their hearts, stir their souls, deepen their compassion, advance their wisdom, and encourage their hope

the sense of home, roots, place, belonging, friends, and family they have found in a significant relational grouping in the congregation

Deliver, strongly, *any two of these four* and people are likely to put up with inadequate parking. But, it raises the stakes on how well we deliver two of these.

A HELPFUL COMBINATION

A helpful combination is sufficient land, attractive landscaping, and adequate parking. This is not to suggest that rural churches should become "citified." Nor is it to suggest that churches in cities should seek to look like their rural counterparts. Rather, it is simply to suggest that people form strong impressions of a congregation in relation to whether or not there is sufficient land, attractive landscaping, and adequate parking. It makes sense, therefore, to pay attention to these possibilities.

Know this: this is not the most important of the central characteristics of strong, healthy congregations. This is the tenth characteristic, appropriately so. There may come a day when parking will not be as critical an issue as it is now. And, at the same time, unless there is a major change in our cultural patterns, people will continue to depend upon automobiles as their principal mode of travel.

The text suggests, *"Let the little children come unto me. Do not hinder them."* My passion is for people, not parking. Insufficient land, poor landscaping, and inadequate parking *hinder.* Inadequate parking does not help. It hinders.

We may, some times, not be able to help a person wrestling with a grievous human hurt and hope. Helping someone who is wrestling with alcohol is a tough one. I am not willing to "get beat" on a simple one like parking. This one is easy compared to helping persons with the complexities of their lives.

Many congregations have a genuine interest in reaching persons on behalf of the grace of God, the compassion of Christ, and the hope of the Holy Spirit. These congregations take seriously the factors of land, landscaping, and parking. They are not complacent. They have a solid balance between land, landscaping, and parking—and worship and generous giving.

Such congregations include parking for occasional worshipers and community persons. All of these persons grow forward their longings and yearnings for the grace of God. They discover the family of the congregation. They share in the mission of the congregation in the world.

Rating Guide: Land, Landscaping, and Parking

Item	Maximum Points	Our Congregation's Rating
1. Our church owns sufficient, usable land for our present life and future mission.	25	____
2. Our landscaping contributes to a first impression of an open and spacious, warm and welcoming, inviting and gracious spirit.	25	____
3. We have adequate parking for our ten major Sundays of the year. (See Chart B.2 in Appendix B.)	25	____
4. We have adequate parking for our normal Sundays and for our weekday use.	25	____
Total	100	____

Instructions

- Use the resources of this chapter to evaluate your congregation's rating in each of the listed items.
- Enter your rating numbers in the blanks. Then, find the total.
- Divide the total of your score by 10 to obtain your congregation's rating on a scale of 1 to 10.
- Enter your rating of Land, Landscaping, and Parking on the chart in Appendix C on page 258.

Further Resources

Building for Effective Mission
The Future That Has Come
Effective Church Finances
The Twelve Keys Bible Study

11

ADEQUATE SPACE
AND FACILITIES

One key, one possibility, for a strong, healthy congregation is adequate space and facilities.

A strong, healthy congregation:

- Has adequate space and facilities for our present and future mission, shepherding, worship services, groupings, and programs
- Has a balance between our land, landscaping, parking, and our space and facilities
- Has space and facilities that are well maintained on a regular basis
- Has space and facilities that create a warm first impression of welcome, being attractive, and helping persons feel at home

For many leaders and pastors, the space and facilities stir fond memories of special events in their lives . . . . weddings, baptisms, special children and youth events, music, worship, Bible study, good fun and good times. Many leaders saw, years ago, some of the facilities when they were new or renovated. They have the picture of "newness" in their mind's eye.

They "almost see" the current worn, tattered condition. They almost "see" the homey, pleasant clutter of stuff, laying around, gathering dust, that hasn't been moved in years. A vast number of leaders and pastors mistakenly assume that the way they see the church is the way everyone sees it. Their own familiarity with the church gets in the way.

Adequate space and facilities give us an opportunity to invite people to a welcoming home. Together, we experience the grace of God and the spirit of family and community.

ADEQUATE

Our congregation has adequate space and facilities for our present and future mission, shepherding, worship services, groupings, and programs.

Many congregations have adequate space and facilities. You can assess whether your congregation does. Analyze the major uses of your current space and facilities and the extent to which they are being used for their maximum possibilities.

One way to do this is to secure a floor plan of your facilities. Mark on it the frequency of use of each of the various facilities on a week-to-week basis. You will be able to determine the:

major uses of the space and facilities during an average week
principal areas of crowding
spaces that are underused
potential uses of space that are yet available

You will discover the extent to which maximum use of your space and facilities is taking place. You will discover ways to advance the full use of your space and facilities.

Some congregations **underbuild** their space and facilities. More churches underbuild than overbuild. For every large church that is uncomfortably empty, there are scores of congregations that are uncomfortably crowded. Many churches limit their growth potential because they underbuild their space and facilities.

They block themselves from the maximum use of their space and facilities. The reason for this is simple. More often than not, the congregation that underbuilds has an original set of plans that is well designed. The giving campaign comes in short. They reduce the square footage of the spaces in the plans until the smaller size now matches the dollars available.

The larger the space, the more uses the space will have. The smaller the space, the fewer uses the space will have. For example, a church school classroom was originally planned to be generously large so it could be used for a wide range of groupings. It was reduced in size to "save money." Its uses are now severely limited. Underbuilding prevents maximum use of space and facilities. A congregation that builds space and facilities that are large and flexible is in a healthier position to use its spaces to the maximum.

We can assess how adequate our space and facilities are with a step-by-step consideration of the specific spaces we have. We can use the following as a checklist.

Worship Home. Our worship home is adequate when it is comfortably filled or comfortably empty. Adequate relates to people's perceptions of comfort. Uncomfortably crowded feels like the worship space is too small. Uncomfortably empty feels like the worship space is too large. Both feel inadequate. A sanctuary can be too small; it can also be too big. Neither condition matches the present and future "fit" for the congregation.

By the same token, many congregations have a worship home that "fits" with the congregation's ten best Sundays. This focus on your ten major Sundays is primary. Then, also consider how your worship home "fits" with the normal Sundays and the weekday uses of the space. Then, think of how your worship space fits with the future mission of your congregation.

Fellowship Hall and Community Life Center. Some congregations have a combined worship home, fellowship hall, and community life center. The one facility serves in these flexible ways. Some congregations have distinct spaces for their worship home, their fellowship hall, and their community life center.

When a congregation has three distinct facilities, it becomes important to assess whether each one is being used to its fullest ability through the whole of the week.

Many congregations have a distinct worship home and a combined fellowship hall–community life center. This combined facility is more feasible for many congregations, from both a land available and a "money invested" point of view. The art is to study the range of activities that your congregation is holding in the spaces. Study the extent to which you are using the spaces richly and fully across an average week. Then, ascertain the present and long-term adequacy or inadequacy of the spaces.

Kitchen. Excellent kitchens serve the current and future interests and activities of the congregation. For many congregations, a "warm up," covered dish kitchen is most adequate—with a refrigerator, stove, microwave, sink, dishwasher, and a range of utensils and dishes. For many congregations, a somewhat more advanced kitchen is most adequate—with sufficient equipment to prepare and cook simple meals.

For many congregations, a complete, commercial kitchen is most adequate—with the kinds of equipment one would find in a commercial restaurant. In recent times, I have seen more and more of the first two types of kitchens and fewer of the third type. Many congregations prefer, for a large group, to have a major meal catered rather than try to prepare it from scratch.

Church School. Excellent church school classrooms have a minimum size of approximately four hundred square feet for every fifteen to twenty persons. It is not that each classroom must have exactly this amount of space. In a given congregation, with twelve classrooms, five church school rooms have this much space, five have more than this amount of space, and two do not have this much space. This is adequate. In another congregation, four church school rooms have this much space, one has more than this much space, and seven have less than this much space. This is verging on inadequate.

What *is* inadequate is building "walk-in closets" and calling them classrooms for children. I see too many classrooms that are too small, both for the children using them and for use by anyone else. It is more helpful to have a few classrooms that are adequate and spacious than to have small walk-in closets. It is more helpful to have five generous classrooms that are adequate. We will look for five excellent teachers and five excellent assistant teachers.

When we have ten small classrooms, with the same total square footage, we now have to find ten self-sufficient, stand-alone, excellent teachers, who will show up each week. Yes, in the five spacious classrooms we will have several interest centers. The five are more effective and less expensive than the ten. We will do well.

Church school classrooms of the future are importantly flexible and highly usable spaces for a wide range of age groups. Given construction costs and energy factors, it is no longer feasible to build church school classrooms that are designed in narrow ways to be used by only one age group.

A given classroom might be used by one age grouping in a specific year. In another year, or several years from now, the same space might be used by another age group. We no longer build spaces so age specific that we close down the future use of the space. A size of approximately four hundred square feet, the size of a two-car garage, is not a hard and fast rule. It is a helpful guideline on which to base judgments as to the adequacy of church school space.

Nursery, Toddler, and Kindergarten. Two factors affect the adequacy of the nursery, toddler, and kindergarten areas: space and design. With regard to space, most churches mistakenly think that since children are smaller than adults, they need less space; they then pick the smallest room that can be found for the nursery, place some cribs very close together, and assume that this will be adequate. This assumption is erroneous. Children frequently need *more* space than adults.

Regarding design, it is important that the congregation's spaces for nursery, toddler, and kindergarten be designed in relation to today's parents rather than the parents of earlier decades of raising children. These spaces need to communicate a sense of security and warmth to today's parents of nursery, toddler, and kindergarten children. It is finally the parents who bring or who do not bring their children to these spaces.

Too many churches have nursery, toddler, and kindergarten spaces designed by adults whose children were young in the 1950s and 1960s but have since grown up. Textures, colors, lighting, and equipment are best secured in consultation with parents who have small children in the current times. Some nurseries communicate that they are simply out-of-date, not because they're really out-of-date, but because they were designed with the textures and colors that were prevalent in an earlier time and are no longer used by parents in the current time.

Storage. It is difficult to describe adequate storage. My good friend, Merrill Douglass, leading time management consultant in the country, has what he calls Douglass's Law of Clutter: *Clutter expands to fill the space available.*

Some congregations have too much clutter and not enough storage. When we open the storage areas, or simply look around the rooms, we find items "forgotten" there, lying around, that have not been "seen" or used in ten years.

We have *adequate* storage when we have these best practices. We store *only* items that have some reasonable probability of being used on a regular basis. We have adequate storage for these items. Sometimes, we store on-site the items we use frequently, from week to week.

We may store our seasonal items on-site, such as Christmas or Easter decorations. We store our once-every-couple-of-years and our once-in-a-long-while items in a member's storage space or we may rent a unit in a mini warehouse. We may have

a "museum" space in our church for cherished items of significant, historical value. We do not store clutter.

Mostly, congregations, even when they have dispersed all
the clutter items, still do not have adequate storage. Think of
chairs and tables. Congregations can have adequate storage
for the chairs and tables that will not be used each day. We do
not use the room itself to stand extra chairs and tables around
the walls of the room. It looks tacky. It looks like more people
"should have come." We have in sight only the chairs and tables
for the grouping using the room at that moment. Regrettably,
many congregations use the room as the storage area. We find
ways to help with this.

I encourage you to consider the range of storage spaces
available. Take into account health and fire precautions in relation
to these storage spaces. Then, consider whether your storage is
adequate.

Restrooms. We consider the adequacy of restroom spaces in
relation to our worship services and our church school groupings. Consider three factors. First, think through whether or
not the restrooms are adequate for our ten best Sundays. Though
there are other times when restroom spaces are in use, our ten
best Sundays usually attract the largest groups of people. Therefore, determine the number of persons your present restroom
spaces can service in a twenty- to thirty-minute period. This
is the amount of time reasonably available before and between
worship services and church school. Then, match this factor
with your worship and church school attendance on your ten
best Sundays.

Second, consider whether some of your restrooms help
handicapped persons, mothers or fathers with small babies, and
small children. We want to be hospitable and welcoming with
persons. We can be thoughtful and generous in simple ways.
Some of our restrooms are helpful to the wide range of persons
we seek to serve.

Third, consider whether your restrooms are attractive, open, clean, spacious, and secure. There is adequate ventilation. There is adequate lighting. They have been recently decorated. There is adequate security. Consider these factors. You will now know whether the restrooms spaces are adequate.

Arrangement. We study the arrangement of the space and facilities. The way the facilities are arranged influences a visitor's perception and a congregation's perception of their adequacy. An adequate arrangement is one that makes the various spaces and facilities easy to locate. The various hallways and corridors are sufficiently large and are arranged to facilitate ease of movement. There are no bottlenecks. There is no jigsaw puzzle. These communicate a negative image even when the space and facilities themselves may be quite adequate.

These guidelines will help you assess the adequacy of specific spaces within your total facilities. Invite two or three persons whose judgment you trust and respect to reflect with you on the adequacy of the church's space and facilities. Select persons who are not familiar with your space and facilities. You will have the chance of learning their first impressions. In that way, you will gain some understanding of the first impression of community persons who visit your congregation for the first time.

Likewise, you can invite two or three persons in the congregation to reflect with you on the adequacy of your space and facilities. You can use the list of spaces in this section of the book as a checklist. With thoughtful conversation, you will discover both where you are and ways to advance.

BALANCE

Our congregation has a balance between our land, landscaping, parking, and our space and facilities.

We are in balance when our space and facilities match with one another in size and capacity of use. The key areas for balance are our worship home, our fellowship hall, our church school classrooms, and our parking.

Frequently, we discover a church plan where the fellowship hall is too small in relation to the size of the worship home. It cannot accommodate the number of people who are likely to participate in activities there in relation to the number of people who participate each Sunday in worship. Sometimes, the worship home is too small in relation to the capacity of church school classrooms.

The ratio of balance will vary from one part of the planet to another and from one congregation to another, depending on the major worship services, congregational gatherings, and community events of a congregation. This is not to suggest that every congregation should have a worship home, church school classrooms, and a fellowship hall. Indeed, many local congregations do not have all three of these facilities.

Flexibility contributes to balance. With the rise in construction costs, loan payments, interest rates, maintenance costs, and utility expenses, it is important that a congregation develop flexible spaces that can be used by a variety of groups. It no longer makes sense to build facilities that are used by one group for a few hours per week. The art of maximum use of space and facilities is greatly helped by developing highly flexible spaces.

This does not mean the groups should be moved around from one space to another year after year. Indeed, many church school classes continue to meet, from one year to the next, in essentially the same space. In the children's division, the practice of promoting the children from one room to a new room was in vogue for a number of years. The notion was that very specialized rooms must be designed for specific age ranges of children.

As churches build increasingly flexible spaces, it becomes important that church school classes and other groups have the sense of a room that is home. Flexibility does not mean shifting a group from one space to another. Rather, flexibility means that several groups share a given space over the course of an average week's usage. It is both more effective and less expensive to have spaces designed in such a way that they can be used by several groupings for twenty or more hours per week.

It helps for a given church school class of kindergarten children to continue to meet in the same space as they are promoted through early elementary school together. We shift the furniture rather than the children. The advantages of giving a group a sense of roots, place, and belonging is an important value, given the highly mobile character of our culture. The group develops a sense of "shared ownership" with other groups who use this flexible space during the week. The generous cooperation among the leaders of the various groups helps this to happen well.

In the years to come, I see many advantages and few difficulties in helping groupings live in and share the same generous, flexible space. The costs make it no longer feasible to build many "single-use" spaces. We develop fewer, more flexible spaces where several groups feel at home. The question is no longer, "What one group owns this one, single-use space?" The focus is now on generous, flexible spaces that several groups can constructively share in the course of an average week.

WELL MAINTAINED

Our congregation has space and facilities that are well maintained on a regular basis.

When we have space and facilities, we acquire four good friends:

regular cleaning
preventive maintenance
ongoing restoration
major emergency repairs

Regular Cleaning. We do this well. Whether we are volunteers, who take turns, or a combination of volunteers and part-time staff, or volunteers and full-time staff, our space and facilities are cleaned on a regular basis. Dust and dirt are not present. Or, they stay for only a short visit. We are not an archeological site. We are a well kept gathering of space and facilities that serve people well.

Preventive Maintenance. Our facilities and equipment are on a schedule of preventive maintenance. A long time ago, we learned it is cheaper to do preventive maintenance than it is to defer it until something breaks down. We look several years ahead and develop a reasonable schedule of consistent, simple, preventive maintenance. We have a team who sees to it that the schedule is achieved.

It is less expensive and more effective to do long-range preventive maintenance for space and facilities than it is to repair them as emergencies occur. And, we put in place a preventive maintenance plan as any new facility is being built. Otherwise, the annual operating budget of the church will be under stress continually from major emergency repairs that must be done unexpectedly and without sufficient reserve funds to take care of them.

This does not mean that a church should invest large sums of money in maintenance. A plan for preventive maintenance enables us to provide thoughtfully and wisely for those items that should be cared for year by year rather than waiting for them to pile up, with the attendant possibility of exorbitant, emergency expense.

Ongoing Restoration. Ongoing restoration is more helpful than capital improvements. When we do ongoing restoration well, we diminish the need for capital improvements. Some congregations neglect ongoing restoration for a number of years. The default: they now have to do a major capital improvements effort. It is more effective and less expensive to practice ongoing restoration.

I was helping one congregation. Forty years before, they had quit taking care of their worship home, education building, and fellowship hall. Not one spot of paint. No "spring cleaning." Each passing year, each passing decade, the three buildings looked worse and worse. Peeling paint. Cracks. Chips. Dirt. Dust. The morale declined lower and lower. The price to fix things up grew higher and higher.

We put in place a seven-year ongoing restoration plan. In year one, we restored the narthex to their worship home and the entry vestibule to their fellowship hall—two highly visible, quick wins. In year two, in the education building, we restored the nursery in the northwest corner and the primary meeting room in the southeast corner. It is a principle I call "cornering the building." This corner looks really good. The opposite corner looks really good. Everything in between looks a whole lot worse. We develop the momentum and the money for year three, year four, and so on. In year seven we do the worship home. In year eight, we start over.

I said to them, "Even if we had all the money to fix all three buildings up in one year, we would not do that. We would then have twenty to thirty years of fading and declining; then, we would have to have another capital funds drive. *The art of facilities is to show something new each year. The older the facilities, the more important it is to show something new each year.* Our ongoing restoration plan helps this to happen."

When we have fourteen rooms, it is more helpful to paint two rooms a year over a seven-year period. We show something new each year. This is more effective than waiting until the paint is nearly falling off the walls and having to do all fourteen rooms at once.

People long for something new. An ongoing restoration plan helps the congregation to experience something "new" each year. Yes, the older a facility is, the more important it is to do this. Congregations desire something new. Sometimes, they become involved in building new, additional space and facilities to satisfy this longing. They may not actually "need" the new facilities, but they are trying to satisfy their longing for something new.

We may be a congregation with modest space and facilities. We may have a worship home, a few classrooms, and a combined fellowship hall–community life center. Our ongoing restoration plan may be on a five-year cycle rather than a seven-year cycle. Well done. To be sure, some major items may be on a ten- to fifteen- to twenty-year cycle, such as a roof or a piece of major equipment. We have a solid ongoing restoration plan.

I encourage you to assess the condition of your facilities and the improvements that might help to put them in good condition. The condition of a congregation's property communicates a strong message about how well the congregation thinks of itself.

Congregations who have developed, for a variety of reasons, low self-esteem tend to neglect their space and facilities. That is not to say that when you find space and facilities neglected you can immediately assume that the cause is low self-esteem. It may be that the financial resources of that congregation have been invested elsewhere in mission outreach.

At the same time, the condition of the space and facilities communicates a strong message to community people about how this congregation thinks of itself. The more adequate the condition and the more straightforwardly the congregation improves its space and facilities, the more likely that community persons think of the congregation as strong and solid.

A building that looks reasonably clean and well kept creates a stronger impression. Further, it encourages a possible standard for homes and other kinds of buildings in the community.

Major Emergency Repairs. There is correlation between the quality of construction and major emergency repairs. We build excellent construction. We deliver cost-effective preventive maintenance. We have fewer major emergency repairs. We use the facilities well, richly and fully. We make maximum use of each space each week. We understand the life expectancy of each specific space, given normal wear and tear.

We do build solid space and facilities. We do not build ornate, elaborate, fancy space and facilities. We do not build "gingerbread" facilities with extraordinarily expensive ornamentation and decor. Our facilities are highly usable and a strong symbol of mission. Our facilities are not a monument to some architect, some pastor, or some group of lay leaders.

We build sound spaces. The roof doesn't leak. The walls are not falling down. You would be amazed at how many roofs do leak and how many walls are falling down. When we build a building, we get to pay on the front end for a solid building, or we get to pay over the years for major emergency repairs. The latter is more frustrating and more expensive.

When we have a major emergency repair, we fix it swiftly. We quickly take whatever bids will help. We do not linger. We do the repair now. We have a people-effective and cost-effective approach to maintaining our buildings.

We have this same people-effective, cost-effective approach when we build a new building or renovate a current building. We take into account:

> the number of persons served in our ten best weeks and in our normal weeks
> the original construction costs
> the interest and principal payments on any loans
> the cost of regular cleaning and utilities
> the cost of ongoing restoration, preventive maintenance, major emergency repairs
> the new giving and the new income the building project is generating and will generate in the years to come

These factors will help us to keep our space and facilities well maintained.

WELCOME .... HOME

Our congregation has space and facilities that create a warm first impression of welcome, being attractive, and helping persons feel at home.

We have distinct "senses" of what home feels like. For our congregation and our community, our space and facilities feel like home.

We look closely at our space and facilities. We decorate with a sense of home, not organization. We think of colors and textures that share a spirit of home, matching with our congregation and the community we serve. People walk in and they feel at home. People experience welcome .... home.

For longtime congregations, this is important. We want our space and facilities to feel at home for today. From time to time, people update their own homes. Or, they move to another home. The key is home. We want both our own home and our congregation's home to "feel like" home. We can look at our space and facilities with the spirit of helping them to be home.

For new congregations in our time, this is especially important. Note well that the first unit shapes all subsequent units. The spirit, size, and shape of the first unit determine the number of people the congregation is likely to serve in its early years. *The more the space and facilities feel like home to the people in the community, the more persons the congregation is likely to serve.*

It helps for new congregations to spend a little longer period of time meeting in temporary facilities, such as a school auditorium. Then, build a substantial first unit that feels like "welcome .... home." In some instances, the first unit may be the only unit the congregation builds. We plan to be a small, strong congregation.

In this case, it is particularly important that the facility be reasonably adequate. In some instances, the first unit is of sufficient size that it will attract an increasing number of people.

The congregation becomes even stronger in its capacity to move on with its plans to build a second unit.

A frequent mistake with a first unit is for the new congregation to try and duplicate a large church plant, only in "mini" form. They try to replicate, albeit on a smaller scale, all of the spaces they hope to have in a final plan. We would not do that. We would build only a few spaces large enough so that we can continue to serve. We do so with as small an investment of money up front as possible. Generally, this means *not* building the worship home first. This is a more expensive space to build per cubic foot than a fellowship hall or flexible classrooms.

Sometimes, when the shape of the land makes it possible, we build a two-story facility, much like a hill barn, with ground-level entrances on both levels. We provide ground-level entries for handicapped persons on each level. Such a facility is generally less expensive in terms of construction costs and utilities than a one-story campus-style building. There are exceptions to this in various parts of the planet, but new congregations can give this consideration.

In the mission culture of the coming years, we build to grow. We do not assume that we must grow and, then, build. Some congregations would grow to an overcrowded condition, then build needed space and facilities to alleviate overcrowded conditions. But, seldom did the congregation build large enough to accommodate the range of community persons with which it could be in mission. Often, a congregation would move into its additional facilities to find it was immediately overcrowded once again.

A congregation that shares one strong mission, shepherding visitation, stirring and helpful worship, and significant relational groupings can overcome the disadvantage of inadequate space and facilities. We deliver any two of these four. We will survive, and thrive, for a number of years. We provide the relational strengths with compelling strength. People put up with being overcrowded.

A congregation that provides, with strength, two of these four, and *also* moves forward to provide adequate space and facilities is a congregation that can build to grow rather than waiting for the growth and, then, playing "catch up ball," trying to build.

People make a house a home. A house does not make a home. People do. Some leaders and pastors get caught up in a building project. They assume that when they have fine, new facilities they will, therefore, have a strong sense of family and community. This is not the case. New space and facilities may provide a momentary source of satisfaction. There is a fleeting moment in which the congregation takes pride in its accomplishment.

But the enduring sources of satisfaction come from the strengths of the relational characteristics of a strong, healthy congregation. The quality of our mission outreach and the quality of our life together, shared with one another and with the community at large, give us a "home," not simply a house. We look for roots, place, and belonging. We associate roots, place, and belonging with given spaces in our own lives. We discover community with a congregation. We sense that these facilities are home for us.

Rating Guide: Adequate Space and Facilities

Item	Maximum Points	Our Congregation's Rating
1. We have adequate space and facilities for our present and future mission, shepherding, worship services, groupings, and programs.	25	_____
2. We have a balance between our land, landscaping, parking, and our space and facilities.	25	_____
3. Our space and facilities are well maintained on a regular basis.	25	_____
4. Our space and facilities create a warm first impression of welcome, being attractive, and helping persons feel at home.	25	_____
Total	100	_____

Instructions

- Use the resources of this chapter to evaluate your congregation's rating in each of the listed items.
- Enter your rating numbers in the blanks. Then, find the total.
- Divide the total of your score by 10 to obtain your congregation's rating on a scale of 1 to 10.
- Enter your rating of Adequate Space and Facilities on the chart in Appendix C on page 258.

Further Resources

Building for Effective Mission
Effective Church Finances
Giving and Stewardship
The Twelve Keys Bible Study

GENEROUS GIVING

One key, one possibility, for a strong, healthy congregation is generous giving.

A strong, healthy congregation:

- Is a congregation of generous people
- Makes available all six sources of giving
- Lives the principles of giving
- Builds on the best practices, the three resources, that contribute to generous giving—giving pattern, assets, and giving family

For many grassroots persons, leaders, and pastors, generous giving is a way of life. They experience the generosity of God's grace in their lives. They experience mentors, family, and friends who help them to live lives of generous grace.

The way they live life is the way they give. They do not "protect and preserve, conserve and hold their meager financial resources." They know God has not done that with them. They know of God's generous grace with them. They are generous givers because God is the generous giver with them.

When we encourage persons to be generous givers, we invite them to confirm God's generosity in their lives. We are generous because God is generous with us. Being a generous giver is not a matter of our having a spirit of good will. Being generous is not, finally, something we do out of our own doing. Being generous is God's gift to us. I think of it this way: "By grace, we are generous givers, and this is not of our own doing, it is God's gift to us."

GENEROUS GIVERS

Our congregation is a congregation of generous people.

God encourages us to live generous lives, to be generous givers. Many congregations have generous givers. They live life with a spirit of generosity. They are generous givers with their strengths, gifts, competencies, and resources. Strong, healthy congregations are generous congregations. Generous people create strong, healthy congregations. Strong, healthy congregations create generous people. Both are true.

Some years ago, the term "generous givers" came to me. The Scriptures lift up the generosity of God's grace. God invites us to be cheerful givers. It is clear. We are not to give out of duty or obligation. We are encouraged to be "cheerful, generous" givers. Since this insight came to me, I have emphasized the gift of generosity, the gift that God gives us to be generous givers.

Strong, healthy congregations never have enough money. They are always living on the brink of bankruptcy. They are always giving away more money than they have . . . . to serve persons in mission . . . . to help persons with their lives and destinies in the grace of God. They are happily generous.

Weak, declining congregations and dying congregations never have enough money. They are always living on the brink of bankruptcy. They are always conserving and holding, protecting and preserving their meager financial resources. Someone, usually on the finance committee, stands and says to the congregation, "We want you to know that the finance committee is doing the best it can to conserve and hold, preserve and protect our church's meager financial resources."

The announcement just taught everyone in the congregation to conserve and hold, preserve and protect *their* meager financial resources.

Three to five persons, with a spirit of generosity, can help a whole congregation to be a generous congregation. Three to five persons, with a spirit of conserving and holding, can help a whole congregation to be a protecting and preserving congregation. It works both ways.

People long to live a life of generosity. They yearn for a congregation that will reinforce in them a spirit of generosity. Strong, healthy congregations reinforce a spirit of generous living. Weak, declining congregations reinforce both a cautious, tentative generosity and a conserving and holding spirit. Dying congregations reinforce a protecting and preserving spirit, struggling to lose no more than they have already lost. They bury their generosity in the ground.

You are welcome to assess the spirit of your congregation. To some extent, this is a subjective enterprise. Do not think too poorly of yourself. Do not thing too highly of yourself. Look at the acts of generosity your congregation shares. Look at the pervasive spirit of your congregation. Consider to what extent your congregation is generous.

Know this. Some people appear to be stingy and selfish. Not true. Wherever you find someone who appears to be self-ish and stingy, you have found a person who has been scarred or scared or both. They are using the behavior of selfish and stingy as a self-protective mechanism to avoid being scarred or scared yet another time. Given half a chance, people have a genuine spirit of generosity.

Share your generosity. You will discover, richly and fully, the generosity with which God blesses you. You grow forward your capacity for generosity. God is generous with us so we can learn to be generous with one another. God encourages us to be generous with one another with the same richness of generosity with which God is generous with us.

Our generosity is not of our own doing; it is the gift of God. We are generous because God is generous with us. This is a matter of grace. We are generous because of the generous grace of God blessing our lives. We are generous givers.

SIX SOURCES OF GIVING

Our congregation makes available all six sources of giving.

People, in our time, share their spirit of generosity in six ways. Sometimes, I call these the six sources of giving . . . . the six giving doors. These are not six ways people *should* give. Rather, I am simply confirming the six ways people do give. You will discover a fuller conversation of these six in my books *Giving and Stewardship* and *Effective Church Finances*. For our current purposes, let me confirm the six:

Sources of Generous Giving

Spontaneous gifts	Generous congregations tend to have three to five invitations a year. Each is a worthwhile cause that directly helps people. People do impulse buying. This is impulse giving. This is an excellent sprinter way of giving.
Major community Sundays	Strong, healthy congregations tend to have ten major community Sundays a year. These include Easter, Christmas, Christmas Eve, plus seven more. There is no special offering. We have the regular offering. Attendance is high; the giving is high. This is an excellent sprinter way of giving.
Special planned	Generous congregations usually have two to four special planned offerings a year. These tend to have an institutional focus, and may be the same causes year after year. This is an excellent sprinter way of giving.
Major project	Strong, healthy congregations have a major project every three to four years. The project may focus on mission, staffing, building improvements, debt reduction, new facilities, or some combination. People share generous three-year pledges to accomplish the major project. This is an excellent sprinter way of giving.

**Annual
giving**

Generous congregations share in giving to the annual budget. Congregations practice pledging, faith giving, tithing, or a combination. This is a solid marathon runner way of giving.

**Enduring
gifts**

Enduring gifts is my term. I look at it through the eyes of the giver. The giver is trying to give an enduring gift, a gift that lasts. Some call this endowment giving. This is looking at the gift through the eyes of the counter. Identify five to eight major enduring gift projects that have balance, integrity, and broad-based appeal. Set a goal for each and a date to achieve the distinctive goals. This is an excellent sprinter way of giving.

Five of the six sources of giving are excellent sprinter sources of giving. In our time, most charitable giving is excellent sprinter giving.

Some congregations close five giving doors, and open only the annual giving door. They reduce the giving of the congregation. For example, a finance committee closes the spontaneous giving door out of the mistaken notion that they want to "protect" annual giving to the budget. People are going to do a certain range of spontaneous giving during a year. With that door closed in their church, they simply shift their spontaneous giving to the Salvation Army, the American Heart Association, and so on.

The rule of thumb is: open all six giving doors. Your total giving will be about three times what your giving is to the annual budget. A congregation was giving $100,000 to their annual budget. Over a period of time, they opened the other five giving doors. Their total giving moved to about $300,000 in generous giving.

Build on your strengths. Encourage the motivations of compassion, community, and hope. Share excellent sprinter and solid marathon runner possibilities of giving. Live as a family, a movement, a congregation, a mission.

You can consider which of these six giving doors your congregation has open. You can think of which giving doors you can open in the coming three to five years. Your total giving will grow.

PRINCIPLES FOR GIVING

Our congregation lives the principles of giving.

Generous congregations live these principles of giving:

Living is giving. Giving is living. The two are good friends. Each helps the other. Each reinforces the other. We live lives of *generous living . . . . generous giving.*

People give to a winning cause. People do not give to a sinking ship. The more we describe ourselves as a sinking ship, the less people give. When we remember *whose* we are, we have the confidence and assurance that we are the Easter People. We are the winningest cause in the galaxies. With humility, we are grateful for the grace of God.

People have a spirit of generosity. This is because of whose we are, not who we are. God's nature is amazing generosity. We are created in the image and likeness of God. Our spirit of generosity is not of our own doing; it is the gift of God.

People live forward to positive expectancies. It is not so much expectations. That has the ring of law. Positive expectancies have to do with possibilities of grace. People do, sometimes, regrettably, live downward to expectations. We can live forward to the positive expectancies we have of ourselves and that others share with us.

People give to people. Then, people give to purposes. Next, people give to programs. Finally, people give to paper—in response to brochures and letters. People are less prone to give to line-item budgets. People genuinely want to help people. There is a flood, an earthquake, a fire, a family tragedy, a compelling cause. The money pours forth to help. Funds are successfully given. The primary reason is that people give to people.

Money follows mission. The stronger the mission, the more generous the giving. It is not that we first find the money and, then, go and do the mission. We find the mission, and the money finds us. We pray, we yearn, we long for the mission. The money comes.

People give out of compassion, community, and hope. These are the primary motivations for generous giving. People do give out of challenge, reasonability, and commitment. The prevailing motivations are compassion, community, and hope. See *The Future That Has Come* for more resources on the primacy of compassion, community, and hope as motivations for generous giving.

Relax, have fun, enjoy life, live in Christ. When we are tense and tight, nervous and anxious, we become conserving and holding, protecting and preserving. We are more generous when we relax and have fun. We live with joy and wonder. We live with new life and hope. Richly, fully, we enjoy the gift of life. We live in Christ. We give.

Consider which of these principles are present in your congregation, and which ones you can put into place during the coming three to five years. Your generosity will grow.

There is a myth that people would rather build buildings than give to mission causes. Frankly, the reason they give for buildings is that the blueprints are specific and concrete.

They can see objectively how their giving is being used. Many congregations are as specific and concrete in developing a blueprint for a mission. People give generously because they can see a clear blueprint for a specific mission that delivers concrete help.

Some congregations send out the following message: "We've gotten a little bit behind on our budget. The utilities were a little more than we thought they were going to be. We've tried to do the best we can. Would you please send us a little money to help us catch up?" That is what people do. They send a little money.

The congregations most effective in encouraging generous giving share this message: "Our church is serving many people. We are delivering concrete, effective help. Your generosity is being shared wisely and well. Thank you for your generous giving." The congregation that approaches the matter in this fashion is given generous giving.

People give to people with whom they have mutual trust, respect, and integrity. People are invited to give to a cause. They decide to give based on two factors: (1) this is a worthwhile cause, and (2) they have mutual trust, respect, and integrity with the persons inviting them to give. Giving is not built on interesting gimmicks or cleverly worded letters. Rather, giving is built on mutual trust, respect, and integrity.

GENEROUS GIVING AND SOLID FINANCIAL RESOURCES

Our congregation builds on the best practices, the three resources that contribute to generous giving:

Giving pattern	we know where we are in our giving
Assets	we know our full assets
Giving family	we encourage our whole giving family to give generously

Strong, healthy congregations share a theology of generosity, a theology of stewardship. Stewardship is generosity. We are stewards of God's grace and generosity. Stewardship is not "saving and conserving." That is not a theology of stewardship. A notion that stewardship is to help a congregation conserve its funds is counter to the Biblical witness. God is lavish with God's grace. As stewards, we are generous with God's gifts.

A theology of stewardship encourages us to be generous in sharing money for mission. It is not the task of the church to save money. It is not the task of the church to spend money. It is the joy of a congregation to generously invest its funds, with compassion, so that mission and lives are advanced. Healthy congregations avoid foolish spending. They avoid foolish saving. They "invest" their funds in generous causes that advance the lives of persons.

Our congregation lives these three best practices that contribute to generous giving and solid finances . . . . to our being generous, strong, and healthy:

Giving Pattern.   First, we know where we are in our giving. We do the giving pattern best practice. We achieve a giving pattern with these steps:

> discover the total giving for each of the recent three years
> chart the giving by each month for each of the three years
> find the percentage of the total giving that was given each
>   month
> calculate three-year average percentage for each month

For example, we may discover that the three-year giving pattern average for January is 6 percent, July is 2 percent, October is 4 percent, and December is 30 percent.

We look to the coming year. We set our giving goals for each month based on our recent three-year giving pattern. For our purposes here, I am illustrating the month of January.

Giving Goal for January

January		Giving Goal for the Year	$100,000
3 years ago:	5%		
2 years ago:	7%		
Last year:	6%		
3-year average:	*6%*	*Giving Goal for January*	*$6,000*

Some congregations share announcements in their newsletters and bulletins.

For January, the notice would read:

January Giving Goal	$6,000
Given	$6,200

Thank You for Your Generous Giving

The notice does not say, "Needed this month." It points to giving, not needs. It points to the behavior we want to encourage, namely, giving. It does not say, "Received this month." That would be looking at the matter through the eyes of the counters, not the eyes of the givers. It says, "Given." We honor what has happened. It does not say, "We are behind." We are not. We are slightly ahead of our giving pattern based on the recent three years.

We do ***not*** divide our yearly giving goal by twelve, and say we need one-twelfth each month.

January		Needed This Year	$100,000
3 years ago:	5%	(1/12 is 8.33%)	
2 years ago:	7%		
Last year:	6%	Needed each month	$8,333
3-year average:	6%	Received	$6,500
		We are behind	*$1,833*

The one-twelfth approach is inaccurate. It does not match the actual giving pattern of congregations. It is unachievable.

Farmers know this. Many vocations know this. Giving patterns vary across the year. People's income patterns vary across the year. The one-twelfth approach creates artificial negative reinforcement. Most congregations receive more than one-twelfth of their giving in December. Using the one-twelfth approach creates eleven losing seasons.

They are called January, February, March, April, May, June, July, August, September, October, and November. Someone usually stands and says, "Woe is us. We are behind." Sometimes, this person has a gentle gift for scolding and uses the one-twelfth approach to scold the congregation yet another month. When a congregation uses the three-year average giving pattern resource, it will accurately and realistically know whether it is ahead, behind, or on target.

Assets. Second, we know our full assets. We practice doing an assets analysis quarterly. Strong, healthy congregations have a full sense of the total assets available to them. Weak, declining congregations have only a partial sense, now and then, of the total assets available to them. Dying congregations are sufficiently preoccupied with what they do not have that they cannot see what they do have.

In strong, healthy congregations, we have a full sense of our total resources. These resources include:

current giving
net new giving
enduring gifts
other assets
potential giving resources

Current giving. Most congregations have more current giving than they think they do. Regrettably, some congregations think of current giving only in relation to giving to their operating budget for the present year. As a matter of fact, congregations receive considerably more contributions in a given year than are designated solely for the operating budget.

A thoughtful analysis of a congregation's financial and giving situation takes into account all the gifts to all six sources of giving. When giving is discussed, we do not discuss only the giving to the annual budget. That leaves out of the picture five sources of giving. It leaves out all of the excellent sprinter sources of giving. We look at our total giving. Many congregations are more generous than they think they are.

Current giving goes up with increased participation, not increased membership. We increase our total giving by increasing two of the first four relational strengths. There is very little correlation between an increase in membership and an increase in giving. Members who do not worship with us tend not to give. The correlation is between participation and giving. People who participate in mission, shepherding, worship, or groupings—any two of these four—tend to give.

Net new giving. When we have one, major, legendary mission in the community, three things happen:

> people are helped with their lives and destinies
> some persons, helped in the mission, decide to become part of the mission
> some persons in the community decide they want to be part of the mission

Our congregation, as a by-product, grows. The net new giving to our congregation grows.

New participants give in about the same giving ranges as current participants. Somehow, they discover, perhaps by osmosis or by informal conversations, the "going giving ranges" present in the congregation. They discover this is a generous congregation. They give generously. They contribute to our net new giving.

With new participants, whether community persons, constituents, or members, look at their total giving. They are more likely to express their generosity through spontaneous giving, major community Sunday giving, special planned giving, major project giving, and enduring giving. The mistake would be to look only at their giving to the annual budget. They will give generously, when invited, to all six sources of giving. They are more likely to advance their giving with the five excellent sprinter forms of giving.

Enduring gifts. The principal of the gift stays intact. It is never invaded. It is never borrowed against. The interest is used to give support to specific enduring causes. My book ***Effective Church Finances*** has a helpful chapter on enduring gifts. Many strong, healthy congregations have enduring gift projects. These enduring gifts can constitute a large source of both giving and of assets for a congregation.

Other assets. Assets are also land, space and facilities, equipment, vehicles, stocks, bonds, and other liquid and capital assets a congregation has gathered over the years. We adequately assess our full financial resources by doing a careful analysis of all the assets we have gathered over the years. Many congregations do not really know the full range and depth of the assets with which God has blessed them. They tend to look only at the annual budget giving. It is helpful for us to look at the whole of God's generosity with us.

Potential giving resources. Strong, healthy congregations look ahead. They have a sense of which of the six sources of giving they are going to develop in the coming three to five years. We may not have all six of the "giving doors" open at the present time. Our giving plan helps us to know which giving doors we plan to open in each of the coming years.

Giving Family Resources. Our third best practice is this: we encourage our whole giving family to share their generosity. Mostly, we do so with spontaneous giving, major community Sunday giving, major project giving, and enduring giving. It is not true that the only people who give to worthwhile causes are members. Look closely. Many people who are not members give generously to causes that help persons and communities with their lives and destinies.

Many congregations have more generous givers than they think they have. The reason some groupings do not give is because no one asks them. A timid, hesitant asking does not help. A harsh, demanding asking is worse. For a worthwhile project, many groupings give generously. The project has value. They are asked with respect and trust, confidence and assurance.

Your congregation's whole giving family includes:

Estimated Number

Leaders, Board, Team Clusters—the informal and formal key leaders of the congregation in mission, shepherding, worship, wisdom, and community

_____

Friends and Family—persons in your congregation's friendship, family, and relational networks that are glad to support specific projects

_____

Mission Project Persons—persons who have participated in or are planning to participate in one or more mission projects related to your congregation

_____

Community Persons—persons in the area, region, and world who think well of your congregation's helpful, legendary mission

_____

Persons Served in Mission—persons helped through your congregation in the recent five years, or at some point in the past

_____

Constituents—nonmembers who participate in some mission, shepherding, worship, grouping, or program activity of your congregation

_____

Members of Your Congregation who
are reasonably active, or who are somewhat
active, or who are our Christmas and Easter   _____
members

Our Giving Family   **Total Possibilities:** _____

I call these groupings "our whole giving family."

Many people give generously to causes of which they are
not formal members. Select a major project that is helpful with
the congregation and the community. You might select a mission
with children in the community. Design it well. Consider the
staffing, volunteers, and resources to advance the project for the
coming three years. Be specific and concrete. Develop a clear
blueprint for mission, staffing, and resources.

When you ask, with confidence and assurance, many in
your giving family will be glad to give generously over the
first three years. As the project proves its worth beyond the first
three years, people will continue their support. Many of these
groupings help frequently with worthwhile, significant projects.
They are not drawn to help us build a tool shed out back. They
are happy to help with a people-centered project that helps a
generous number of persons with their lives.

Strong, healthy congregations are generous people, make
available all six sources of giving, live the principles of giving, and
build on the three resources for generous giving and solid finances.
These congregations are generous givers. They share gifts of grace.

Rating Guide: Generous Giving

Item	Maximum Points	Our Congregation's Rating
1. The people of this congregation are a generous people.	25	_____
2. Our congregation makes available all six sources of giving.	25	_____
3. Our congregation lives the principles of giving.	25	_____
4. Our congregation builds on the best practices, the three resources that contribute to generous giving: giving pattern, assets, and giving family.	25 _____	_____
Total	100	_____

Instructions

- Use the resources of this chapter to evaluate your congregation's rating in each of the listed items.
- Enter your rating numbers in the blanks. Then, find the total.
- Divide the total of your score by 10 to obtain your congregation's rating on a scale of 1 to 10.
- Enter your rating of Generous Giving on the chart in Appendix C on page 258.

Further Resources

Giving and Stewardship
Effective Church Finances
Twelve Keys for Living
The Twelve Keys Bible Study

CONCLUSION: MISSION, SACRAMENT, GRACE

MISSION

Good Friends. Mission and Grace are good friends. Grace stirs mission. Mission stirs grace. We experience the grace of God and find ourselves sharing mission. We share our longings for mission, and discover the grace of God. The grace God gives us . . . . the mission God gives us . . . . both are gifts of God. People who long for grace share in mission.

Grace is the beginning of mission. Without grace, there is no mission. Mission without grace is dead and dull, gimmicks, gadgets . . . . our vain whistlings in the dark to build our own "stuff."

With grace, mission is alive, timely, helpful, generous, giving. People are helped to discover whole, healthy lives in the grace of God. Grace is mission. Wherever there is grace, there is mission. Wherever there is mission, there is grace.

Someone once wrote, "If you want to build a ship . . . . don't first drum up people together to collect wood, and don't assign them tasks and work, but rather first teach them to long for the sea." My saying is: "If you want to build a mission congregation . . . . don't first drum up people together to hold meetings, and don't assign them tasks and work, but rather first teach them to long for the grace of God."

We begin with grace. We end with grace.

We pray with grace. We plan with grace.
We act with grace. We serve with grace.
We live with grace. We become grace.

God's reforming acts of grace and mission touch the whole of humanity. It is not that God reforms the church and then, the church reforms the culture. That assumption is a latent archeological relic of that long-ago notion that the church is the primary source of grace in humanity. God is the primary source of grace. God chooses to speak directly to humanity through acts of grace and mission.

Mission Growth. God invites us to mission growth. Mission growth congregations begin with the question, "Who is God inviting us to serve in mission?" Mission growth congregations focus on mission growth more than church growth. The question is not, "Do we want to grow?" The question is, "Who is God encouraging us to serve in mission?

We are a mission growth congregation:

We begin with, "Who is God inviting us to serve in mission?"
We share the five basic qualities of strong, healthy congregations.
We claim the **Twelve Keys** strengths with which God blesses us.
We expand, add, sustain our strengths.
We act swiftly to serve God's mission.
We live whole, healthy lives in the grace of God.
We pray, deeply, richly, fully, with our whole being.
We have fun, as the Easter People, living in the wondrous grace of God.

Among the Scriptures that enrich, inform, and shape mission growth congregations is this:

One day he got into a boat with his disciples and said to them,

"Let us cross to the other side of the lake."

So they set sail.

Luke 8:22

We learn as much from what the text does not say as by what it does say. No one said, "Let us stay here." No one suggested, "Let us plan before we go." No one timidly mentioned, "Let us stay near the shore." No one pleaded, halfway across, "Let us turn back."

The gift of grace in the text is: *"So they set sail."* God invites us to set sail. Mission growth congregations set sail.

Where we begin shapes where we are headed. Mission growth congregations are strong, healthy congregations, living in the grace of God, serving well in God's mission. Many congregations are part of the mission growth movement. For these congregations, the focus is: We are helping the persons God is inviting us to serve in mission. We are a serving congregation.

We serve for the sake of serving. We do not serve to grow. We share mission for the sake of mission. We do not do mission to grow. The goal is serving, not growing. When we serve, sometimes we grow. Then, we give thanks to God twice, once for the serving and, then, again, for the new persons who have joined with us in the serving.

In the end . . . . God invites us to mission growth. In the Last Judgment questions, there is no question about: Did you grow a bigger church? Did you build a bigger building? Did you have a bigger attendance in worship? All of the questions in the Last Judgment are mission questions: feeding the hungry, clothing the naked, sharing the Gospel with the poor. In the end . . . . the questions will be about mission growth.

Some congregations suggest that once they stop the decline, once they grow, once they get to a certain size, then they will be able to turn their attention to mission growth. In the meantime, they simply change their terminology. They call church committees mission teams, but they continue to behave like committees. They seek the illusion that they are really doing mission.

Later, once they have solved the problems of their decline, then they will consider doing something in mission. Amnesia sets in. The frenzied flurry and fury to halt the decline takes over. Rules and regulations proliferate. Ministry standards, complex criteria, and professional evaluation tools abound. Scolding and scaring join in.

These various efforts want to "do good." They "mean well." But, sadly, the preoccupation seems to be on growing bigger churches. The focus seems to be on the data and demographics, graphs and charts, gimmicks and gadgets, tricks and trivialities of how to "get bigger."

Mission growth congregations are willing to risk their existence for a worthwhile cause . . . . a compelling mission of compassion, community, and hope. Some congregations do not do so. They say, "Let us get a little bigger; then, we will be better able to help." That time never comes.

A malaise had fallen across the land.
A time of shadows and sadness.
Woe is us.
We are doomed.

Grace stirs the land.
A time of joy and wonder.
Give thanks to God
We are saved.

God invites us to mission growth. Help your congregation to live in the grace of God, with a spirit of mission, compassion, community, and hope. You will discover a deeper quest than "getting bigger." You will discover the rich, full world of mission growth.

Your longings and yearnings will be stirred. Your compassion for people will be deeper. Your life will be richer and fuller. You will live in hope. Your life will count. You will be a blessing to many. You will be blessed with the grace of God, the compassion of Christ, and the hope of the Holy Spirit.

There is an ancient text, sometimes found in Holiday Inns and Motel 6s. It says something about, "Whosoever would save his life must first lose it for my sake and the Gospel's sake." The text applies to congregations as well as to individuals. "Whatsoever congregation would save its life must first lose it for my sake and the Gospel's sake." God invites us to mission growth.

SACRAMENT

Living. Living is a sacrament. Life is a sacrament . . . . a gift of grace from God. An act of living is an act of grace, compassion, community, and hope. In the act of living, we experience the grace of God. We share compassion. We are community. We live in hope.

As we build on the strengths with which God blesses us . . . . as we expand a current strength and add a new strength, we live out sacramental acts of grace. We touch the lives and destinies of persons with gifts of grace. This venture . . . . this adventure is about sacramental acts of grace, compassion, community, and hope. We experience new life.

We live in grace. People around us live in grace. People across the planet live in grace. This is about more than "getting bigger." This is about living with a sacramental spirit of grace.

There is no way
        We can be sure
                What day will bring
                        What night will stir
We do know this
        Blest with God's grace

Each day we live
Each night we pray

God blesses us with sacramental grace. God blesses us with sacramental living.

Mission. Mission is a sacrament. Sharing mission is a joyful, encouraging sacrament, blessed of God. Mission is not a solemn command or a stern challenge. With mission, we live life with a generosity of spirit. With mission, we rejoice in the grace of God.

The Kingdom of God is like a wedding feast, a great banquet.
    Our sacramental mission feels like a wedding feast, a great banquet.
We are the Christmas people, the People of wonder and joy.
    Our sacramental mission has a spirit of wonder and joy.
We are the People of the Cross, the People of compassion and generosity.
    Our sacramental mission has a spirit of compassion and generosity.
We are the Easter People, the People of new life and hope.
    Our sacramental mission has a spirit of new life and hope.

We experience sorrow and grief .... desolation and loneliness. We find ourselves in sin and worse. Depravity and despair overtake us. Remorse .... regret accompany us. No joy. No wonder. No life.

We share times of celebration .... gatherings of family .... accomplishments and achievements .... wondrous discoveries .... cherished moments .... happiness and joy. We live .... we give. We give .... we live. Our living nourishes us. Our giving restores us.

We are joyful . . . . we have fun . . . . we live a joyful, encouraging, sacramental life of mission, blessed of God. We are the People of the Sacrament of Mission.

GRACE

The heavens are telling of the glory of God . . . . Psalm 19:1. The glory of God is the grace of God. The heavens are telling of the grace of God. The glory of God . . . . the grace of God is immense. God creates the universe as immense . . . . as vast as it is so we will know how immense . . . . how vast God's grace is for us. The immensity of the heavens teaches us the immensity of the grace of God.

The stars are a sacramental sign of how immense God's grace is for you.

On January 1, 1925, a friend read Edwin Hubble's research paper to the gathered astronomers of the planet. Prior to that date, virtually all astronomers agreed: the universe is the Milky Way. Seminars were held, papers were read, debates were conducted, and research projects were explored. All concluded: the Milky Way is the whole of the universe. There is nothing beyond.

With Hubble's insight, we began to discover there is more to the universe than the Milky Way. From 1925 to 1990, we discovered ten billion galaxies. From 1990 to 2000, with the help of the Hubble telescope, we discovered 125 billion galaxies . . . . the number grows each day.

Good friends, it is not "the force be with you." It is "the grace of God be with you." The heavens tell the glory . . . . the grace of God . . . .

We now know our solar system is moving from the constellation Columbra toward the constellation Hercules at 12 miles per second . . . . 720 miles per minute . . . . 30 million plus miles per year. On August 11, 2009, Julie and I celebrated being married for fifty-three years. At that time, we had traveled 1,590,000,000 miles together. It is a wonderful journey with Julie.

We have this confidence. When loneliness, emptiness, lostness slip in, the vastness of God's grace fills our hearts. When fear, anxiety, anger rush in, grace quiets . . . . stills our troubled feelings. When despair, depression, despondency weigh us down, grace lifts our spirits.

We have this assurance. When grudge, resentment, bitterness sap us . . . . wither us, grace strengthens our souls. When hurriedness and confusion crowd in upon us, the grace of God gives us peace. When sadness and tragedy overwhelm us, grace comforts us. Grace restores our souls.

Grace is like drenching rains on a parched, thirsty desert, like the laughter and joy of family and friends gathered for a wonderful birthday. Grace is like a gentle breeze that cools a hot, summer day, like a quiet conversation among two people who dearly love one another. Grace is like spring-filled streams rushing to fill rivers and oceans, like the rich, deep satisfaction of a work well accomplished . . . . well done.

We have this assurance . . . . the grace of God forgives our anxieties and anger, our lamentings and complainings, our resentments and grudges. Grace frees us from hasty actions . . . . harsh words. Grace helps us to forgive and to accept forgiveness. Grace comforts us with peace, quiets us with presence, stills our worries with reassurance.

Grace blesses us with humility and kindness. Grace helps us to be gentle and wise, loving and hopeful. Grace gives us an encouraging, calm spirit. We are grateful for the quietness of peace, for the love of family. Grace makes each day so much easier . . . . so much more fun. We discover good fun . . . . good times . . . . birthdays . . . . anniversaries . . . . graduations . . . . celebrations. We discover loving friends, prayers of comfort, lives generously lived.

We experience rainbows of grace . . . . cooling rains of compassion . . . . gentle breezes of hope. We laugh and love . . . . share and enjoy life. We draw close together as family. The grace of God blesses our communion. God blesses us with the bread of grace . . . . the cup of compassion.

Peace and contentment . . . . goodness and mercy follow us all the days of our lives. We dwell in the house of the Lord forever.

The heavens are telling of the grace of God. Thanks be to God. God bless you. Amen.

. . . . and God said, Behold, I make all things new. . . .
REVELATION 21:5a

A TWELVE KEYS CELEBRATION RETREAT

Gather your congregation for a Twelve Keys Celebration Retreat. The more people you gather, the stronger the ownership for where you head. I have included a possible schedule. Feel free to advance it to meet your own setting. See *The Twelve Keys Leaders' Guide* for further resources.

Our Congregational Gathering

We look forward to sharing a good time together.
> We encourage everyone to come.
We have good fun as we pray and sing, plan and share.
> We invite as many people as possible.

We plan for grace .... strengths .... compassion .... mission ....
> We share possibilities and planning,
> > wisdom and common sense.

We discover the strengths with which God blesses us.
> We discover current strengths to expand.
> > We discover new strengths to add.
> > > We sustain our current strengths.

We look for the strengths to expand and add to which God is inviting us, that we have fun achieving, that are worthwhile, and that stir our compassion, creativity, and hope.

We share a wonderful gathering, a family reunion.
> We sing and pray.

We share simple, generous food. We have a grand party, with
> joyful decorations.

We enjoy good fun and fellowship.

8:00   Coffee, tea, water, juice, donuts, pastries, fruit

8:30   Welcoming, singing, praying

8:45   **Step 1: We claim our strengths.**
        Select your team partner. Decide your lead strengths
        among the *Twelve Keys.*

9:00   Find two other teams. Listen for their wisdom. Share
        your wisdom.
        As a small group, as best good friends can, decide
        which of the *Twelve Keys* are your current strengths.

9:30   We listen for the wisdom from the other small groups.
        As a small group, we share our wisdom with
        the whole gathering.

> As each group shares their wisdom, a
> leader, using "hash marks" on newsprint
> or an overhead, marks our current
> strengths.
> On our own *Twelve Keys* chart, we
> underline once the whole group's
> wisdom as to our current strengths.

Singing, praying, thanksgiving for the strengths God
gives our congregation.

10:00   Break — coffee, tea, water, juice, dessert, fruit

10:30   **Step 2: We expand one or two current
        strengths.**
        With your team partner, select one or two current
        strengths to expand that you know would be fun
        to achieve and would be a helpful gift to the
        community.

10:45   Find two other teams. Listen for their wisdom. Share your wisdom.

As a small group, as best good friends can, decide which one or two of your current strengths would be fun to expand and would be helpful.

11:15   We listen for the wisdom from the other small groups. As a small group, we share our wisdom with the whole gathering.

> As each group shares their wisdom, a leader, using "hash marks" on newsprint or an overhead, marks our current strengths to expand.
> On our own *Twelve Keys* chart, we double underline the whole group's wisdom on the one or two current strengths to expand.

Singing, praying, thanksgiving for the strengths God gives us to expand.

11:45   **Step 3: We add one or two new strengths.**
With your team partner, select one or two new strengths to add.

12:00   Over lunch, find two other teams. Listen to their wisdom. Share your wisdom.
As a small group, as best good friends can, decide which one or two new strengths we can add that we would have fun achieving and would help us to be a strong, healthy congregation.

1:15   We listen for the wisdom from the other small groups. As a small group, we share our wisdom with the whole gathering.

> As each group shares their wisdom, a leader, using "hash marks" on newsprint or an overhead, marks our new strengths to add.

On our own *Twelve Keys* chart, we circle
the whole group's wisdom on the one or
two new strengths to add.

Singing, praying, thanksgiving for the strengths God
gives us to add.

1:45   Blessing

We have gathered and shared our compassion and wisdom . . . .
claimed the strengths God gives us . . . .
decided current strengths to expand . . . .
discovered new strengths to add . . . .
shared good fun and family together . . . .
sung and prayed,
asking God's blessing . . . .

We know where we are headed . . . .
we give thanks to God.
The tradition we are beginning . . . .
is sharing gifts of grace each year
with our whole congregation.

CHARTS

Chart B.1 Maximum "Comfortably Filled" Seating Capacity Formula

1. Main floor seating capacity.   ————
   Omit the front pew unless a railing is present.

2. Choir seating capacity.   ————

3. Balcony seating.   ————
   Reduce total for lack of line of sight.

4. Overflow and transept seating.   ————
   Count overflow back room in rectangular church.
   Count transept side rooms in cross-shaped church.
   Reduce figure for lack of line of sight.

5. Total gross seating capacity (add 1–4)   ————

6. Comfortably filled is 80% of the amount in line
   5 in cities, towns.   ————
   Comfortably filled is 60% the amount in line 5 in
   rural areas.   ————
   Our worship space has:
   Wide center aisle (or double aisles)
   Wide side aisles
   Large vestibule
   Comfortable chairs or short pews (seating 8 or fewer)
   Spacious chancel

7. Reduce the comfortably filled amount in line 6 by
   4% each for the lack of any of the characteristics
   mentioned in 6 above.   ————

Chart B.2 The Number of Available Parking Spaces

1. On-site parking, directly on the property of the
    church, adjacent to the main buildings of the
    church.   _____

2. Nearby parking owned by the congregation,
    with full right of use.   _____

3. Off-street parking owned by someone else with
    whom the congregation has a formal or
    informal agreement to use it.   _____
    Note: Count only the first and second floors
        of decked parking.

4. Off-street parking owned by someone else
    with whom the congregation has no formal
    or informal agreement to use it, but "borrows"
    its use, hoping for the best.   _____

5. On-street parking within reasonable walking
    distance (1–3 blocks), available for use by anyone.
    Reduce on-street parking figure by 40, 50,
    or 60% to ascertain likely available parking.   _____

Add together the figures in 1–5 to ascertain total
available church parking.   _____

Chart B.3 The Annual Giving Value of Your Parking Spaces

This is how to discover the annual giving value of your parking spaces.

1.   This is the number of parking spaces we
     use each Sunday.   _____ spaces

2.   This is the total giving to all causes this year. $ _____

3.   Divide the number of parking spaces into
     the amount of total giving to discover the
     annual giving value of each parking space. $ _____

Example: 70 parking spaces   Total giving: $70,000
            Annual value of each
            parking space is: $1,000
            20 new parking spaces is: $20,000
                                                     annual giving
                                                     increase

The question is not: "How much does the land cost?"
The key question is: "What is the value of the land to us
in the years to come?"

We discover the value of our current parking. We divide the number of parking spaces we are using into our total congregational giving to all causes for the current year. We get a figure. This figure is the annual giving value of each current parking space.

Then, we multiply the annual giving value per space by the number of new spaces we are providing. We discover the new net giving income for the year.

When the new giving income is greater, over a five- to eight-to ten-year period, than the cost of the land, we buy the land. In some downtown areas, we gulp and buy the land, knowing we will be able to realize our investment in fifteen to twenty years.

TWELVE KEYS ACTION PLAN

Our *Twelve Keys* action plan may be a streamlined three pages long.

Following is the outline for your *Twelve Keys* action plan. You can use the following three pages to create your plan.

We claim our strengths   *page one*

On the *Twelve Keys* chart, we underline once our current strengths.

The chart is page one of our action plan.

We expand one of our current strengths.   *page two*

On page one, the *Twelve Keys* chart, we double underline the current strength we plan to expand.

On page two, we state the two to four specific key objectives that will expand this current strength. We may think of ten to fifteen possibilities. The art, what takes wisdom, is to select the two to four that are the 20 percenters. For each key objective, we state, as best we can, who will do what, by when, to achieve each objective.

We add one new strength.   *page three*

On page one, the *Twelve Keys* chart, we circle the new strength we plan to add.

On page three, we list the four to six key objectives that will add this new strength. We may think of ten, fifteen, or twenty possibilities. The art, the wisdom, is to select the four to six that will deliver this new strength. For each key objective, we state, as best we can, who will do what, by when, to achieve each objective.

Twelve Keys to an Effective Church
Strong, Healthy Congregations Living in the Grace of God

page one

Relational Characteristics

1. one mission outreach
by congregation in community
1 2 3 4 5 6 7 8 9 10

2. shepherding visitation
in congregation and community
1 2 3 4 5 6 7 8 9 10

3. stirring, helpful worship
grace centered, well done
1 2 3 4 5 6 7 8 9 10

4. significant relational groupings
home, roots, place, belonging
1 2 3 4 5 6 7 8 9 10

5. strong leadership team
leaders, pastor, staff
1 2 3 4 5 6 7 8 9 10

6. solid decision process
simple organization
1 2 3 4 5 6 7 8 9 10

Claim your current strengths
Expand one current strength
Add one new strength
Act on your plan

Functional Characteristics

7. one major program
among best in community
1 2 3 4 5 6 7 8 9 10

8. open accessibility
in location and people
1 2 3 4 5 6 7 8 9 10

9. high visibility
in location and people
1 2 3 4 5 6 7 8 9 10

10. land, landscaping,
and parking
1 2 3 4 5 6 7 8 9 10

11. adequate space and facilities
spacious, well cared for
1 2 3 4 5 6 7 8 9 10

12. generous giving
solid financial resources
1 2 3 4 5 6 7 8 9 10

underline strengths (8s, 9s, 10s)
underline a second time
circle a 1–7 to grow to an 8
decide your one-time actions

We expand one of our current strengths.   *page two*

We plan to expand this current strength _____

On the *Twelve Keys* chart, we double underline the current strength we plan to expand. On page two, we state the two to four specific key objectives that will expand this current strength.

Key Objective 1.

_____

_____

Key Objective 2.

_____

_____

Key Objective 3.

_____

_____

Key Objective 4.

_____

_____

We add one new strength.   ***page three***

We plan to add this new strength _____

On the **Twelve Keys** chart, we circle the new strength we plan to add. On page three, we list the four to six key objectives that will add this new strength.

Key Objective 1.

_____

_____

Key Objective 2.

_____

_____

Key Objective 3.

_____

_____

Key Objective 4.

_____

_____

Key Objective 5.

_____

_____

Key Objective 6.

_____

_____

ACKNOWLEDGMENTS

I am deeply grateful to the thousands of congregations, their members, and their pastors for their rich insights and helpful experiences. They have contributed greatly to my understanding for developing strong, healthy congregations.

The *Twelve Keys* books have lives of their own. They find their way to leaders, pastors, and congregations whom we will never have the pleasure of knowing personally. The books help countless congregations in the United States, Canada, Australia, and New Zealand. They are helpful with congregations in Europe, Russia, Central America, and South America. Indeed, the books are helping congregations across the planet. Years ago, some were translated into Korean .... a language in Africa .... a language in South America .... Mandarin Chinese.

It is amazing how helpful the *Twelve Keys* books are with congregations of all constituencies, shapes, and backgrounds—small, medium, large, mega, rural, small town, large city, and metropolitan—across the planet. Julie and I are grateful the *Twelve Keys* books help so many congregations.

As the books have traveled the planet, an extraordinary range of leaders, pastors, and congregations have been kind to share their insights and discoveries. Countless congregations have shared excellent ideas and good suggestions. I am most humbly thankful to all of them.

We have learned much. Further research and experience have come to pass. ***Twelve Keys to an Effective Church, Second Edition, Strong, Healthy Congregations Living in the Grace of***

God shares new suggestions, possibilities, and ways forward for this new time and beyond.

I want to thank Jossey-Bass and the extraordinary team of persons gathered there: Sheryl Fullerton, executive editor; Debbie Notkin, contracts manager; Alison Knowles, senior editorial assistant; Joanne Clapp Fullagar, editorial production manager; and Michele Jones, copyeditor. Each of them has given excellent wisdom and encouragement to this new work. I am grateful for their gifts, thoughtfulness, and insight.

This book, *Twelve Keys to an Effective Church, Second Edition, Strong, Healthy Congregations Living in the Grace of God; The Twelve Keys Leaders' Guide, An Approach for Grassroots, Key Leaders, and Pastors Together;* and *The Twelve Keys Bible Study* join the *Twelve Keys* family of resources for congregations. I am grateful for the gifts and competencies with which the leadership team of Jossey-Bass has brought these new books to publication.

I am grateful to our older son, Ken, who has been kind enough to create a new Web site, www.twelvekeys.org. There, you will discover helpful possibilities for seminars, speaking invitations, consulting resources, and *Twelve Keys* planning retreats. You will find ways to order the books and to register for major seminars I lead each year. You will discover some pictures of our family.

Julie and I are most grateful for the wonderful persons across the planet with whom we are friends and family. God bless you all.

                                                      Kennon L. Callahan, Ph. D.

SPECIAL
ACKNOWLEDGMENTS

I want to share special acknowledgment and thanks with these good friends. They have been most encouraging and helpful in advancing this new work. It has been a joy and pleasure to share with them. Our conversations together have been most helpful. Their insights and wisdom, their compassion and hope have advanced the book a thousand fold. I am deeply and humbly grateful to them. They are a wondrous group of friends.

Rev. Jonathon Chute is Senior Pastor with Rolling Hills United Methodist Church in Rolling Hills Estates, California. He loves working with people to discover the grace of God in everyday, ordinary life. He especially enjoys helping the congregation to live out its mission in a time when many people do not see organized religion as a part of their lives. He knows that this is a time when the community of faith can make a real difference in the world, and is grateful for the chance to be a part of it. Jonathan studied Comparative Religion at Harvard University and received his M.Div. from Pacific School of Religion in Berkeley. Before coming to Rolling Hills, he served congregations in Pacific Palisades, California, and London, Ontario, Canada. He lives in Palos Verdes Estates with his wife, Dr. Thyra Endicott, and their daughter, Hannah.

Karen Horst, Dip. C.E., B.A., M.R.E., M.Div., began her ministry in the Presbyterian Church in Canada as a regional educational consultant resourcing congregations and developing leaders. She then represented her denomination in church school curriculum design and writing. Karen has written many study guides and courses. Most recently she has completed a series of online courses for several denominations cooperating together. As a minister of Word and Sacraments, she has served a midsize and large congregation and also worked as an Interim Minister. Her great passion is international development and aid. She has traveled extensively in this capacity. Her other passion is assisting congregations in strategic planning and conflict resolution. Karen, most recently, is enjoying her new grandchildren. One of Rick and Karen's greatest joys is that they were married by Dr. Kennon Callahan.

Rev. Bill Britt is the Senior Minister of Peachtree Road United Methodist Church in Atlanta, Georgia. He is a graduate of Stetson University in DeLand, Florida. Bill received his Master of Divinity degree from Candler School of Theology, where he was a student of Dr. Callahan, and his Doctor of Ministry degree from United Theological Seminary. He is married to Wendie, and they have two children, Sara and Will.

Rev. Rick Horst has been a minister within the Presbyterian Church in Canada since 1984, serving inner-city, small town, and urban congregations over that time. Currently pastor of St. Andrew's Church, Barrie, Ontario, he continues to share his interests in strategic planning, mission growth, and stewardship with other congregations and denominations beyond his own, as time allows. He holds a Bachelor's degree from the University of Waterloo, an M.Div. from Knox College, Toronto, and the Doctor of Ministry degree from McCormick Theological Seminary in Chicago. Married to Karen, they share a love of grandchildren, motorcycling, and cottage life.

Sara Myers is one of the three founding members of settingPace, LLC, a publishing services company that serves the educational publishing community. Since her introduction to the *Twelve Keys* in 1994, she has adapted and applied them to the business setting. Sara lives in Cincinnati, Ohio.

Rev. Jim Cairney is the Lead Pastor in Christ Church–The United Church of Canada, in suburban Mississauga, Ontario, west of Toronto. He is the author of *Along The Emmaus Road, Walking With The Risen Christ* (United Church Publishing House, 1994). Born in Montreal, and raised in Lancaster, Ontario, Jim has a Bachelor of Applied Arts in Journalism from Ryerson Polytechnical Institute (now Ryerson University), Toronto, and an M.Div. (Honours) from St. Andrew's College, Saskatoon, Saskatchewan. An award-winning journalist, he was the full-time Religion Writer for *The Hamilton Spectator* from 1985 to 1988. Ordained in the United Church of Canada in 1981, he has served in a number of places and contexts across Canada, including rural, isolated, and new church development. Jim believes passionately in the mission and ministry of congregations in our day. His lead spiritual gift is hospitality. He enjoys cooking, sailing, skiing, canoeing, swimming, music, and theatre. He and his wife, Ann McRae, have two adult sons, Joel and Aaron, and the great joy of a grandson, Robert Cairney-Barnes.

Rev. Richard Lee Worden was born and raised in Pikeville, Kentucky. He is a graduate of Kentucky Wesleyan College, Candler School of Theology, Emory University, and received an Honorary D.D. from Emory and Henry College. He is a member of the Virginia Conference and founded St. Stephens Methodist Church in Springfield, served appointments at South Roanoke United Methodist Church, was Senior Minister of Annandale UMC and of Reveille UMC in Richmond, and was District Superintendent of the Alexandria and Roanoke Districts of the United Methodist Church. Richard retired in 1999 after serving forty-one years in the Virginia Conference. Richard and his wife, Elizabeth, have three daughters (three great sons-in-law!) and eight grandchildren.

Ken Callahan Jr., personally, is the proud husband of Shay and the father of three sons, Blake, Mason, and Brice. The family enjoys all outdoor activities from snow sports to water sports, sailing and rock climbing, under the watchful eye of Shadow, the family's devoted Labradoodle. Professionally, Ken is a graduate of Emory University's Goizueta Business School. He has held leadership roles in Brand Management and Supply

Chain Management with Reebok, Vuarnet, Body Glove, O'Neill, JanSport, adidas AG, i2 Technologies, and SAP AG, applying the *Twelve Keys* principles in business. Presently, Ken is one of two founding partners of KED Consulting, focused on strategic opportunities to improve a Brand's Organization and Supply Chain.

I am grateful for all of their helpful insights and suggestions. I take full responsibility for the final work.

Kennon L. Callahan, Ph. D.

ABOUT THE AUTHOR

Kennon L. Callahan, B.A., M.Div., S.T.M., Ph.D., is grateful to be the husband of Julia McCoy Callahan, his best friend and beloved wife. An honored researcher, professor, and pastor, Dr. Callahan is today's most sought-after church consultant and speaker. Author of many books, he is best known for his groundbreaking *Twelve Keys to an Effective Church*, forming the widely acclaimed Mission Growth Movement, helping congregations across the planet.

Thousands of congregations and tens of thousands of church leaders and pastors around the world have been helped through his writings and workshops.

His seminars are filled with compassion, wisdom, encouragement, and practical possibilities.

He travels extensively, speaking to groups of pastors and key leaders from the United States, Canada, Australia, New Zealand, South Africa, and many other parts of the world.

An Ordained Elder in the United Methodist Church, Dr. Callahan taught for many years at Emory University. His fields of research and teaching include theology of mission, leadership and administration, and giving and finance.

Dr. Callahan is the founder of the Center for Continuing Education at Emory's Candler School of Theology. He is the founder of the National Certification Program in Church Finance and Administration, providing training and certification for pastors and church administrators. He has received many awards and recognitions, including being elected to the Hall of Fame of the National Association of Church Business Administrators.

Dr. Callahan is the founder and Senior Fellow of the National Institute for Church Planning and Consultation. Dr. Callahan is the founder of the Mission Growth Movement.

His pastoral experience spans rural and urban congregations in Ohio, Texas, and Georgia, and includes small, strong congregations, healthy middle congregations, and large, regional congregations.

Dr. Callahan has earned the B.A., M.Div., S.T.M., and Ph.D. degrees.

> Bachelor of Arts, Kent State University, major in Philosophy, double minors: Religion and Psychology
>
> Master of Divinity, Perkins School of Theology, Southern Methodist University, Systematic Theology, Historical Theology, and Sociology of Religion
>
> Master of Sacred Theology, Perkins School of Theology, Theology of the Church and the Leadership and Administration of Congregations
>
> Doctor of Philosophy, Emory University, Systematic Theology, the Nature and Mission of the Church

Dr. Callahan and his wife, Julie, have two sons and three grandchildren. They share a love of the outdoors, music, quilting, dogs, astronomy, reading, traveling, geology, and sailing.

Three New Books by Kennon L. Callahan

Twelve Keys to an Effective Church, Second Edition, Strong, Healthy Congregations Living in the Grace of God

The five basic qualities for strong, healthy congregations. Plus, new possibilities for the *Twelve Keys* to an effective, successful congregation. New suggestions for expanding your current strengths and adding new strengths. New wisdom and insights for mission, sacrament, and grace. The book helps you to be a mission growth congregation.

The Twelve Keys Leaders' Guide, An Approach for Grassroots, Key Leaders, and Pastors Together

Momentum. Resources. Strengths. The book helps you build the momentum of your congregation, deepen the resources of your congregation, and advance the strengths of your congregation. Your congregation will develop a strong, healthy future. The book shares excellent ideas and good suggestions on how to lead a helpful Twelve Keys Celebration Retreat. The book provides resources for encouraging momentum and action. It shares insights on the dynamics of memory, change, conflict, and hope. The book is an excellent companion for the new *Twelve Keys* book.

The Twelve Keys Bible Study

The book shares the Biblical resources for the *Twelve Keys*. It shares scriptures for each of the *Twelve Keys* and reflections on these scriptures. It shares suggestions and questions for study and conversation. This resource is helpful for Advent and Lenten Bible studies, Sunday School classes, small group studies, and for preaching and worship services. The book is an excellent companion Bible study for the new *Twelve Keys* book.

The Future That Has Come

The seven major paradigm shifts of recent years. New possibilities for reaching and growing the grassroots. Motivating and leading your congregation.

Small, Strong Congregations

Ministers, leaders, and members of small congregations develop a strong, healthy future together.

A New Beginning for Pastors and Congregations

What to do in the first three months of a new pastorate; how to make a new start in a present pastorate.

Preaching Grace

Pastors develop an approach to preaching that matches their own distinctive gifts.

Twelve Keys for Living

People claim the strengths God gives them and develop a whole, healthy life. Solid Lent or Advent study.

Visiting in an Age of Mission

Develop shepherding in your congregation. Groupings to shepherd. The variety of ways you can do so.

Effective Church Finances

Develop an effective budget, set solid giving goals, and increase the giving of your congregation.

Dynamic Worship

Major resources for stirring, inspiring worship services, helpful and hopeful in advancing people's lives.

Giving and Stewardship

How to grow generous givers. Motivations out of which people give. Six primary sources of giving. Giving Principles in generous congregations. How to encourage your whole giving family.

Effective Church Leadership

Foundational life searches. Seven best ways to grow leaders. Develop constructive leadership.

Building for Effective Mission

Develop your mission. Evaluate locations. Maximize current facilities. Building new space. Create an effective building team. Selecting an architect. Develop an extraordinary first year.

Twelve Keys to an Effective Church, Strategic Planning for Mission

Claim your current strengths, expand some, and add new strengths to be a strong, healthy congregation. Encourage your whole congregation to study this book—it helps in their church, family, work, and life.

Twelve Keys: The Planning Workbook

Each person contributes directly to creating an effective long-range plan for your future together.

Twelve Keys: The Leaders' Guide

How to lead your congregation in developing an effective plan for your future. How to develop action, implementation, and momentum. Dealing with the dynamics of memory, change, conflict, and hope.

Twelve Keys: The Study Guide

An excellent bible study of the *Twelve Keys,* with helpful resources and solid discussion possibilities.

INDEX